BLACK COUNTRY
CHAPELS

NED WILLIAMS

SUTTON PUBLISHING

Sutton Publishing Limited
Phoenix Mill · Thrupp · Stroud
Gloucestershire · GL5 2BU

First published 2004

Copyright © Ned Williams, 2004

Title page photograph: Providence Baptist
Chapel at Bell End, between Rowley Regis
and Blackheath, 2004. *(NW)*

British Library Cataloguing in Publication Data
A catalogue record for this book is available from the
British Library.

ISBN 0-7509-3990-7

Typeset in 10.5/13.5 Photina.
Typesetting and origination by
Sutton Publishing Limited.
Printed and bound in England by
J.H. Haynes & Co. Ltd, Sparkford.

THE BLACK COUNTRY SOCIETY

The Black Country Society is proud to be associated with **Sutton Publishing** of Stroud. In 1994 the society was invited by Sutton Publishing to collaborate in what has proved to be a highly successful publishing partnership, namely the extension of the ***Britain in Old Photographs*** series into the Black Country. In this joint venture the Black Country Society has played an important role in establishing and developing a major contribution to the region's photographic archives by encouraging society members to compile books of photographs of the area or town in which they live.

The first book in the Black Country series was *Wednesbury in Old Photographs* by Ian Bott, launched by Lord Archer of Sandwell in November 1994. Since then 55 Black Country titles have been published. The total number of photographs contained in these books is in excess of 11,000, suggesting that the whole collection is probably the largest regional photographic survey of its type in any part of the country to date.

This voluntary society, affiliated to the Civic Trust, was founded in 1967 as a reaction to the trends of the late 1950s and early '60s. This was a time when the reorganisation of local government was seen as a threat to the identity of individual communities and when, in the name of progress and modernisation, the industrial heritage of the Black Country was in danger of being swept away.

The general aims of the society are to stimulate interest in the past, present and future of the Black Country, and to secure at regional and national levels an accurate understanding and portrayal of what constitutes the Black Country and, wherever possible, to encourage and facilitate the preservation of the Black Country's heritage.

The society, which now has over 2,500 members worldwide, organises a yearly programme of activities. There are six venues in the Black Country where evening meetings are held on a monthly basis from September to April. In the summer months, there are fortnightly guided evening walks in the Black Country and its green borderland, and there is also a full programme of excursions further afield by car. Details of all these activities are to be found on the society's website, **www.blackcountrysociety.co.uk**, and in *The Blackcountryman*, the quarterly magazine that is distributed to all members.

PO Box 71 · Kingswinford · West Midlands DY6 9YN

CONTENTS

Introduction 5

1. Bricks & Mortar 13

2. Anniversaries 15

3. Banners 19

4. Tin Tabernacles 25

5. Missions & Mission Halls 31

6. The North-East Frontier 39

7. Willenhall and Darlaston 45

8. Wolverhampton 49

9. Bilston 57

10. Hell Lane to Sodom & Up the Bonk 63

11. Through the Villages 69

12. Tipton 77

13. Woodside: Anniversaries & the Boys' Brigade 87

14. Netherton: More Chapels than Pubs 91

15. Cradley & Cradley Heath 103

16. Brierley Hill: Chapels on A Tea Towel 117

17. Contrasts in The Lye 133

18. Blackheath, Old Hill & Halesowen 137

19. The Salvation Army 141

Acknowledgements 144

Let's build a chapel! A great step towards fulfilling that dream is the moment the foundation stones are laid. It's 1928 and the congregation at Cradley Forge Chapel, Quarry Bank (New Connexion), lay the foundation stones of their new Sunday School building at Hammer Bank. Their existing chapel was below Hammer Bank in the valley of the River Stour, but ten years later worship transferred to the Sunday School building and has been there ever since. The debt incurred in erecting the building was paid off with the profits of the amateur dramatic presentations put on in the hall – until a minister banned them as 'un-Christian' in their content. The lad with the trowel is Vernon Pewton, who later lost his life during the Second World War.

Many chapels have bricks inscribed with the names of the members of the congregation who subscribed to the chapel-building fund, as well as the foundation stones laid by better-off sponsors. *(Joyce Parkes collection)*

INTRODUCTION

The Black Country is a restless ever-changing landscape. Local people believed that it would be dominated forever by factories, industrial townscapes, and areas of dereliction and waste created by mining. To everyone's surprise that landscape was ephemeral too, and since the 1960s we have watched as the Black Country has become increasingly green and and increasingly 'suburban'. No ingredient of the Black Country landscape is safe – steel works can be replaced with shopping malls, opencast mining can be replaced with housing estates, little communities can be swallowed up in urban sprawl.

As the Black Country became industrialised and urbanised, its population grew dramatically. Every need of that population had to be met – whether it was a need for a place to have a drink and discuss pigeon racing, or a spiritual need. All the facilities provided to meet the population's needs then became victims of the very

Members of the Macefield Mission parade their banner along Halesowen Road, Old Hill, just before the First World War. All the buildings on the left have now been demolished and the Wesleyan chapel on the right is abandoned. However, the Macefield Mission survives and celebrates its centenary in October 2004, and somewhere beneath the Mission Hall the banner lies buried! *(Kathleen Green collection)*

process of change that had created them in the first place. Nothing is here to stay in the Black Country.

This book looks at the world of chapels. While this book is being produced a number of chapels are closing. Already many have disappeared, or been put to new uses. Therefore part of this book's purpose is to alert readers to what they may have already missed, or forgotten to record. But its other purpose is to demonstrate what still survives and what can still be enjoyed, whether you would still like to witness a traditional Sunday School anniversary, or stumble upon a mysterious chapel that has barely adjusted to the second half of the twentieth century, let alone contemplated moving into the twenty-first.

For the purpose of this book the word chapel is interpreted fairly loosely. For some people the word simply describes a small church, for others the word is used only to describe the places of worship built by dissenters and nonconformists. In both situations the word church is now frequently used, and this adds to the confusion. In this book the parish churches of the Church of England and the churches of the Roman Catholics are ignored even if small enough to warrant the description chapel. For most of this book I look only at the buildings used by other denominations. The exception is the mission church, to which a complete chapter is devoted, on the grounds that they are somehow very chapel-like!

The next problem to be faced is that chapels are numerous and this book cannot consider every chapel. The book's aim is to be selective in a representative kind of way – bringing your attention to past and present, obvious and obscure, architecturally splendid and architecturally nondescript. I have striven to cover a range of denominations and to provide a reasonable geographical spread. Similarly, I have tried to provide a variety of exterior and interior pictures, and to portray the huge variety of human activities that have surrounded chapels. Already, I find myself hoping that a Volume Two can follow this book, to provide more coverage of the subject.

Some of our Anglican churches have histories that predate the industrialisation and urbanisation of the Black Country, but many chapels appeared just as that dual process started to change the old landscape forever. In some instances the Church of England was slow to respond to the changes, and chapels seemed to spring up more quickly than churches. By the middle of the nineteenth century the Anglicans and nonconformists were competing for the souls of the Black Country, and within the nonconformist world there many splits and factions, which made the competition ever more complex.

The earliest chapels or meeting houses to built in the Black Country were built by dissenters in the seventeenth century. These were predominantly Presbyterian, but there were identifiable Baptist congregations in Netherton and Walsall. Visitors to the chapel at Netherend today are reminded that part of the building was erected as early as 1796 when the congregation moved from what had been called the 'Pensnett' Meeting House at Cradley Forge (Pensnett because the meeting house was on the southern frontier of Pensnett Chase). By the middle of the eighteenth century congregations like those at Netherend were calling themselves Unitarian. The very church-like building in Old Meeting Lane, Coseley, may be built in the gothic style that was popular in the 1870s and 1880s, but the Unitarian congregation traces its history back to 1662, and still calls its building the Old Meeting.

The Unitarians and the early Baptists were making steady progress in the Black Country when suddenly, in the 1740s, an Anglican reformer and preacher arrived in the area to change everything forever. This was John Wesley (1703–91). His preaching led to the formation of Methodist societies, which after his death broke away from the Anglican Church and formed the new mainstream of nonconformity. In some places 'Queen Elizabeth slept here' is proof of historical pedigree, but in the Black Country 'John Wesley came here' is of much more importance. When Primitive Methodism was created in about 1820 in North Staffordshire it quickly spread to the south of the county, and to be able to say that 'Hugh Bourne preached here' was of parallel importance.

The Baptists also became more interested in proselytising. New congregations were established as the result of missionary work, and also as a result of congregations splitting and forming breakaway groups – a process that continued right into the twentieth century.

John and Marion Dunn proudly stand by the flagstone on which John Wesley stood when he came to preach in Cradley High Street on 19 March 1770, now preserved in the Cradley High Town Ragged School, Mapletree Lane, Cradley. On the 200th anniversary of the event local preacher Wesley Perrins preached from beside this memorial, thus linking it two more recent home-grown legendary figures of the nonconformist world. (See pages 113–14.) *(John James)*

In the nineteenth century the situation was bewildering as a result of factionalism within the nonconformist world, but the twentieth century has been characterised by re-unification. Some of this re-unification has been a pragmatic response to the decline of chapel and church attendance, and can be seen as a rationalisation of the chapel world. Black Country folk seem to have particularly liked the independence of their nonconformist churches, and there are some interesting examples of congregations preferring to go-it-alone than to amalgamate.

Denominations that began by being evangelical and radical tend to mellow and become more mainstream. Therefore by the end of the nineteenth century a wave of independent mission halls and gospel halls began to appear. A good example is the Fenton Street Mission of Brierley Hill, which still celebrates its survival and independence in William Street. Other examples are featured in the book.

A handbill announcing the foundation stone ceremony at Short Heath in 1881. The people listed on the handbill would make large donations (£25) and would lay a substantial stone. Poorer supporters would buy an individual brick (up to £5), later incorporated into the wall of the building. Many chapels still have rows of named bricks, which have often weathered better than the foundation stones!
(Bill Poole collection)

In the twentieth century further waves of evangelism created new denominations and new chapels, but as we move into the twenty-first century the very word chapel seems out-dated. The Black Country now has its share of 'Christian Centres' and faith-backed multi-purpose buildings, sometimes converted, sometimes purpose built, that defy categorisation. While some Anglican and Methodist congregations appear to be in terminal decline, Pentecostal and a new wave of evangelical congregations seem alive and well.

Naturally I would like to stress the individuality of every Black Country chapel, but nevertheless most chapels do have a history that runs along similar lines. Which came first: the chapel or the congregation? In most cases the answer is quite clear: the congregation came first. Like-minded people would gather in each other's homes to study the Bible, join in prayer, and plan missions. Out of such a society, or class, or meeting would develop the plans to provide a purpose-built building, and the fund-raising would begin. Each step becomes part of the early history of each chapel: the purchase of land, the laying of foundation stones and eventually the opening and dedication of a new chapel, followed by tea parties! Each step provided impetus for further fund-raising, and gathering new followers. Very few new chapels began life free from debt, but all started with abundant enthusiasm.

A Sunday School was usually developed in parallel with the chapel. In some cases the Sunday School would have to be held in the chapel, but the urge to provide separate accommodation was strong. In the first half of the nineteenth century the school could engage in the secular activity of teaching basic literacy and mathematics for people of all ages as well as promote Bible study and prepare children to join the faith. Some ventured in to providing day schools and the Ragged School movement promoted the extension of education to those most likely to miss such opportunities. Eventually this led to much argument about who should provide education: the churches and chapels, or the state?

A pre-war wedding at Mount Pleasant Wesleyan chapel in Quarry Bank? Not quite – things aren't always what they seem in the world of Black Country chapels!

In this case the Youth Club are staging a mock wedding: all the chaps are wenches and all the wenches are chaps! The year is 1946. (*Chapel Archives*)

After the passing of the 1872 Education Act many school boards had to lease Sunday School buildings to provide secular education while the new board schools were being built.

The provision of accommodation that could be used for purposes other than worship led to the flowering of many social and semi-religious activities, which could be developed alongside chapel-going. Most chapels developed activities that occupied every night of the week, ranging from specialist groups for men, women, young women, youth and children. Groups could undertake bible study, train and prepare further Sunday School teachers, or could cover a range of cultural and social activities. Choirs and bands were abundant, but so were football teams and drama groups. Often the activities were contentious – football was OK but not if played on the Sabbath; dramatics were OK but dangerous if they became too secular! The Cradley Forge Operatic and Dramatic Society was so successful that its productions soon paid for the church building, but eventually a minister realised that the presentations could not have official approval and the society had to separate from the chapel in which it had developed. At Woodsetton in 1932 the trustees and stewards of the church were alarmed to find that the Girl Guides were indulging in dancing and the boys at the Jolly Club were boxing!

Chapels were best at creating organisations that reflected their own religiously inspired values. A typical such organisation was the Band of Hope, a national Temperance movement founded by Jabez Tunnicliff in the 1840s. Earlier in his life he had led a split from the Baptist church in Cradley at which he was the minister, and had established a new congregation at Cradley Heath (Four Ways). Another organisation was Christian Endeavour (founded by Dr Francis Clarke in 1881) which made scriptural study into a competitive sport!

The Anti-Cigarette League, which was popular at some chapels, was fairly unsubtle about its moral stance, but far more ambiguous was the practice, also very popular, of having a chapel May Queen, which seemed to combine a pagan tradition with the modern values of a beauty contest. St Cuthbert's at Coseley eventually went right down the beauty contest road and looked forward to the annual parade of contesting beauties in their swimsuits!

This book cannot discuss the theological differences, ritualistic practices and so on of all the denominations meeting in the Black Country. In the past these differences have been very important, but the modern trend has been towards tolerance of each other's differences, and towards a spirit of working together as Christians. All chapels provide a 'from the cradle to the grave' service to their members and alongside the weekly business of prayer and worship there are baptisms, blessings, religious education of children, marriages and funerals, and care of groups with every special need. Some of these activities can be illustrated in this book, while others are difficult to record. The study of chapels embraces everything from baptism to Bible Crusades, from the Band of Hope to the chapel's football team or amateur dramatics society.

In the absence of a Sunday School, the Methodist chapel at Mount Pleasant, Quarry Bank, now holds a Sunday School reunion for 'old scholars', rather than a Sunday School anniversary. This picture records the event held on 19 May 2002. *(NW)*

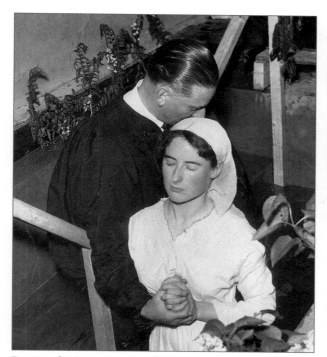

Baptism by immersion. *Left:* Pastor Cove baptises Sylvia Jones at the Seagars Lane Mission Hall, Brierley Hill, May 1954. *Right:* Pastor Lloyd Abel at the Restoration Bible Church, meeting in Providence Chapel, New Road, Willenhall, prepares for baptism fifty years later. *(Author's collection)*

Pastor H. Powell blesses a child at All Saints, Parkfield, Wolverhampton, 18 July 2004. *(NW)*

Many chapels established branches of the Band of Hope – a temperance organisation that asked people to sign the pledge and renounce the evils of alcohol. One Black Country connection with the Band of Hope is that one of its founders, Jabez Tunnicliffe, was a Baptist minister who led a congregation first in Cradley and then in Cradley Heath.

This Band of Hope shield was awarded to successful chapels in the Cradley Heath area and was instituted in memory of Frank Woodhouse whose picture appears on the shield. He was particularly associated with Graingers Lane Methodist Chapel.

Below: Cradley Forge Sunday School football team, Quarry Bank, look pleased with themselves after winning the league in 1937. *(Chapel Archives)*

1 Bricks & Mortar

Black Country chapels come in a variety of architectural styles. The first wave of chapel building in the first half of the nineteenth century produced buildings which generally conformed to classical simplicity – plain and very rectangular. A natural stress of the perpendicular arose from providing a building lofty enough to accommodate a gallery. Providence Chapel from Darby End, now to be found in the Black Country Living Museum, is a good example of this no-nonsense approach.

As the nineteenth century progressed the Victorians developed a love of the Gothic style when it came to public buildings such as churches. This spread to the world of chapels and some chapels forgot their austerity for a moment in trying to be church-like in appearance. The Old Meeting House in Coseley is a good example (see page 69).

In the 1890s and 1900s a remarkable number of chapels were built using red brick and stone-coloured terracotta dressings to create a very distinctive style found all over the Black Country. These were followed by some pleasant inter-war buildings such as the Tabernacle Baptist Chapel in Wolverhampton (page 51) and the superbly built People's Mission Hall in Swan Street, Netherton (page 101) – replacing their original tin chapel.

Post-war chapels and late twentieth-century chapels are still perhaps too new to be appreciated, but many do not seem to have matured very well. Some have proved more difficult to maintain than their predecessors.

The enemy of the Black Country chapel is not Satan but rather mining subsidence. Dozens of chapels collapsed and had to be replaced because they began to tilt or subside, either because they were directly undermined by the search for coal, or were close enough to workings to be affected. In more recent times declining congregations and mergers have led to the abandonment of chapels, and some of the buildings have been put to new uses. One or two have survived by being passed on to new congregations.

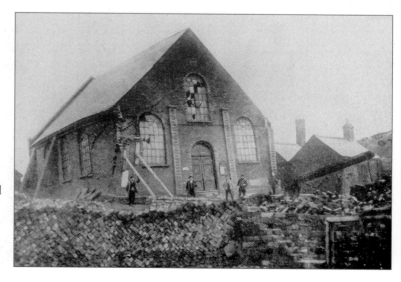

A very faded picture of the first chapel built at Primrose Hill, Netherton, which had to be replaced in the late 1880s (see page 98). The Congregationalists in Dudley had resolved in 1849 to build missions in the 'districts of the poor', which were likely to be districts where the quest for coal most threatened buildings. Cracked walls, leaking roofs and tilting were problems faced by dozens of chapels.
(Albert Willetts)

If you think you've seen this chapel before somewhere you could be right. It is now preserved at the Black Country Living Museum. G.F. Perkins photographed Providence New Connexion Methodist Chapel at Darby End, Netherton, in 1910. It was opened on 29 January 1837 and was later sold to the Primitive Methodists. It is a typical Black Country chapel and has earned its place at the museum. Horace Smith, an elder at Providence, closed the building in 1978, and his son, an architect, had the pleasure of resurrecting it at the museum, where it was re-dedicated on 15 September 1979. *(Albert Willetts collection)*

The Bethel New Connexion Chapel, Garratt Street, Harts Hill, still stands for those keen enough to go in search of it. Built in the 1850s, it closed in 1963 and has since been used as a nut and bolt warehouse. *(NW)*

2 Anniversaries

Undoubtedly a major event in the chapel calendar and way of life was the Sunday School anniversary. This was an annual ritual, celebrated at churches and chapels all over the Black Country and far beyond, but preparations for the event began long before the big day. Perhaps the degree of preparation frightens off modern churchgoers, but in the past it created a tremendous build up to the anniversary. Everyone invested an enormous amount of preparation in the event.

Places on the Sunday School platform during the anniversary service were often in such demand that some chapels had to ration them on a one-per-family basis. If you took part last year, this year your younger brother or sister might take the place. If you failed to take part in all the practices or could not dress properly for the occasion you might have had to forfeit your place.

The practices began weeks before the anniversary and you were expected to learn all the hymns by heart. (Some modern services supply the words on home-made autocue devices improvised with overhead projectors and acetate sheets!) If you were asked to do a solo, reciting a poem or a religious text, then that would entail learning the words, and much practising in the art of projecting one's voice.

Meanwhile Mum or older sisters would be working in the costume department manufacturing a new white dress, or re-sizing an existing dress that had been used before. There would also ribbons to buy for the girls and ties for the boys. The boys would make do with white shirts, but would be expected to look as smart as their female counterparts – by whom they were usually out-numbered. Blue sashes and blue ribbons were frequently featured. Photographs reveal just how uniform everyone looked, although the girls were usually quite clever about introducing an element of individuality to their costume.

Perfect symmetry! An anniversary picture, believed to be the Cranmer Methodists, Whitmore Reans, Wolverhampton, in 1951. (*John Hughes collection*)

Dad and older brothers would be recruited about one week from the anniversary. Their job was to build and decorate the platform on which the Sunday School scholars would sit. This was usually a custom-made piece of joinery – brought out of the storeroom just once a year and assembled with much argument about the order in which pieces had to be put together. In some chapels the platform was a very complicated device, stretching from the choir stalls out into the hall. In other chapels and churches the ordinary seating provided adequate accommodation. Seating was going to be at a premium on the big day.

When the platform was complete there was usually at least one more rehearsal just to practise getting everyone on and off the platform and in and out of their seats. It was also essential that every child rose and took their seat again in perfect unison – usually directed by the choirmaster or Superintendent. One of the worst things that could happen was that you might have to be removed from the platform very publicly if you suddenly wanted to go to the toilet. Almost as serious a crime was the disgraceful possibility of nodding off.

After all the preparation it was quite possible to present up to three performances on Anniversary Sunday. Dads and uncles and grandparents often came to the morning service while mums slaved away preparing Sunday Lunch. Mums and aunts favoured the afternoon service, which was their opportunity to show off a new hat. And then for good measure everybody might come to the evening service, even if it was 'standing room only'.

The parade was another feature of the anniversary, often led by a band provided by the Scouts or the Boys Brigade, and sometimes another opportunity to collect funds. The parade played a major part in reminding a community of the existence of its local chapel – their demise is a serious loss to everyone.

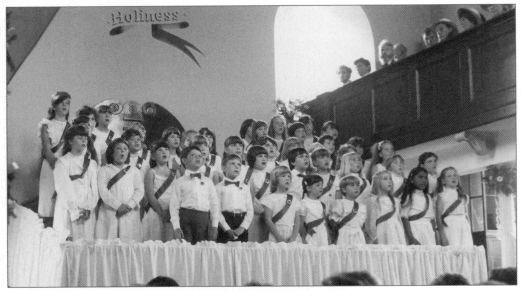

The traditions of the Sunday School anniversary are preserved at the chapel at the Black Country Living Museum. Children from Hopkins Street Chapel, Burnt Tree, are included in those taking part in this 1980s photograph. *(Ray Anstis/Hopkins Street archive)*

The traditions of the Sunday School anniversary parade re-created at the Black Country Living Museum, 11 July 2004. The Sunday School scholars, in white dresses, follow the Scout band down to the museum's chapel – moved to the museum in 1979 from its original location in Northfield Road, Netherton (see page 14). *(NW)*

Another chapel tradition preserved by the Black Country Living Museum is the PSA or Pleasant Sunday Afternoon. The PSA movement, started in Birmingham in 1887, believed that non-chapelgoers might be enticed into chapel for a Sunday afternoon event based on the pleasures of lively hymn singing and fellowship. On 9 May 2004 the PSA welcome committee includes Les and Margaret Millington, Brian and Moreen Wilkes, Alan and Jean Carter, Alan Hallman and Margaret Allen. *(NW)*

The Sunday School parade was a chance for everyone associated with the event to take to the streets – not just the youngsters! Members of the congregation from St Cuthbert's Mission parade through Brookland Grove, Coseley, in the 1960s (see also pages 34–5). *(Ray Baggott collection)*

A traditional platform photograph taken at St Cuthbert's Mission, Coseley, in the 1960s, featuring white dress, sashes and floral decoration. *(Brenda Parry via Jerry Clarke)*

3 Banners

Sunday School banners are one of the forgotten features of local chapel history, and now that Sunday School street parades are almost impossible to organise we may never see their like again. We have forgotten how important it was to acquire a banner, and how much pride there was in carrying one through the streets. Warrington Walking Day, on the first Friday of July, may be one of the last events in Britain where Sunday School and church banners can be experienced *en masse*. There is no Black Country equivalent.

The banners themselves had much similarity to those used by Trade Union branches and Friendly Societies, and the archetypal designs for such banners were established commercially by George Tuthill & Company, the country's leading banner manufacturer. They were at their most popular from the early 1890s through to the First World War. Some chapels, of course, prided themselves on making their own banner.

The Band of Hope and other similar organisations (The Rechabites and Christian Endeavour, for example) also made banners that could be given as an annual trophy to successful branches. Where have they all gone? The answer is that they were fairly fragile and great care was needed in providing proper storage. If wind damage did not destroy a banner, then mildew and rot or vermin would attack it while stored in its box. They seem to survive best when kept on display in dry conditions.

The banner from the Messiah Baptist Church Sunday School, Cinder Bank, Netherton, was donated to the Black Country Living Museum some time ago. 'Feed my lambs' was a popular Sunday school theme on banners, but the origins of this banner seem obscure. It is not in the George Tuthill style. *(NW)*

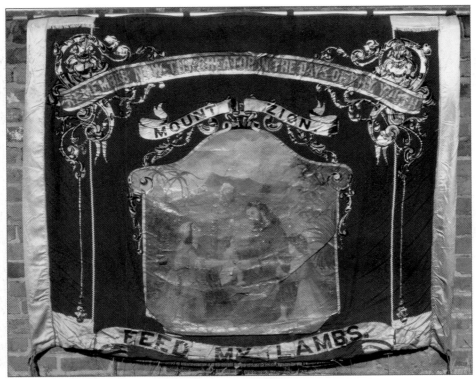

'Feed my lambs' is repeated on this banner from one of the Zion chapels that is now part of the Black Country Living Museum's collection and is in poor condition. The scroll reads 'Remember now thy creator in the days of thy youth'. As in several local banners, the picture does not seem to be of the same standard as the rest of the banner. *(NW)*

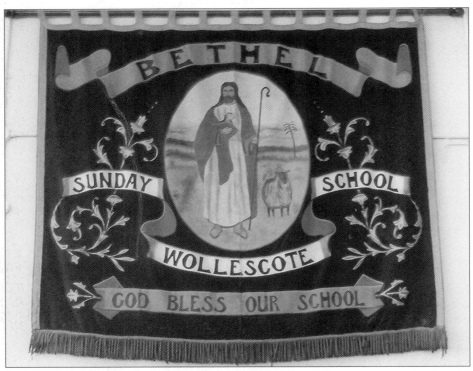

The Bethel Chapel in Hill Street, The Lye, still displays its excellent and colourful banner, May 2004. *(NW)*

The Hurst Hill Wesleyan Methodist Sunday
School banner is still displayed at the annual
Sunday School anniversary. It was
photographed on 30 June 2002 when the
chapel itself was celebrating its 200th
anniversary. *(NW)*

Right: Mrs Thomas stands in front of the
Waterfall Lane Mission Hall's banner that was
bought by the break-away Tory Street Mission
in 1912. The latter is now the Grange Road
Mission and is still home to this magnificent
banner in the George Tuthill style. 'Feed my
lambs' appears on the reverse. The photograph
was taken in June 2004. *(NW)*

The banner at Short Heath is a typical modern home-made banner and is rather hidden in one of the chapel's narrow corridors. *(NW)*

The banner at Noah's Ark Chapel in Netherton was proudly displayed at the chapel's closure on 14 March 2004, but is seen here two weeks later, outside the Sunday School building. Left to right: Rita and Graham Faulkner, Brian Handy and David Willetts. *(NW)*

The People Mission Hall in Swan Street, Netherton, still displays its banner in the Sunday School building. It was photographed here when used at the Sunday School Celebration on 16 June 2004. (See page 101.) *(NW)*

The High Town Ragged School, Cradley, take their banner on the annual Sunday School Parade in the mid-1950s. Some years later they opened their banner box to find it had rotted away. *(Marion Dunn collection)*

The wind catches a Sunday School banner during a pre-First World War parade in Cradley Heath while passing St Luke's parish church at the Four Ways. Cradley Heath seems to have been a centre of church and Friendly Society parades. *(Muriel Woodhouse collection)*

The Methodists from Gorsty Hill set out on a 1930s Whit Sunday Sunday School procession with their banner, probably taking part in a Sunday School treat shared with other schools in the Blackheath area. It appears to be a professional George Tuthill banner. *(Jim Brookes via Anthony Page)*

4   Tin Tabernacles

Sheets of corrugated iron were a Black Country product and therefore it is particularly appropriate that some of our local chapels were tin tabernacles, although there is no record of where the iron sheets that were part of the kits supplied to build such chapels came from.

A leading supplier of such building kits was William Cooper in London. A page from one of his catalogues is reproduced here, and we know for certain that the People's Mission Hall in Swan Street, Netherton, was built in a few weeks in 1898 using such a kit.

They were cheap and easy to build and could be remarkably cosy inside, although rain on the roof was a rather noisy distraction. Many congregations regarded them as temporary accommodation until something more solid could be built. Now they are an architectural endangered species.

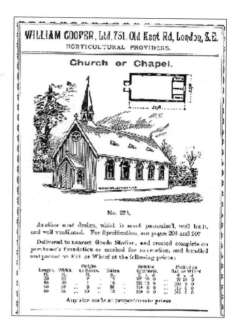

The Italian Pentecostal congregation of the corrugated iron chapel in Gorsebrook Road, Wolverhampton, pose for the camera in July 2002. It was acquired second hand from the Church of England who had used it as a mission church, and there are now plans drawn up to replace it with a modern building. *(NW)*

Tin tabernacles were usually lined with wood panelling or boards. Firms like William Cooper also supplied pews, altars, pulpits, etc., all of which enabled the chapel to be 'up and running' very quickly. In July 2002 we find the Italian Pentecostal congregation inside their chapel in Gorsebrook Road, Wolverhampton. *(NW)*

Trinity Methodist chapel in Church Street, Netherton, occupied a corrugated iron building from 1893 to 1912, after which the building was re-erected at Gornal Wood as the Alexandra cinema (see pages 96–7). *(Cyril Wright collection)*

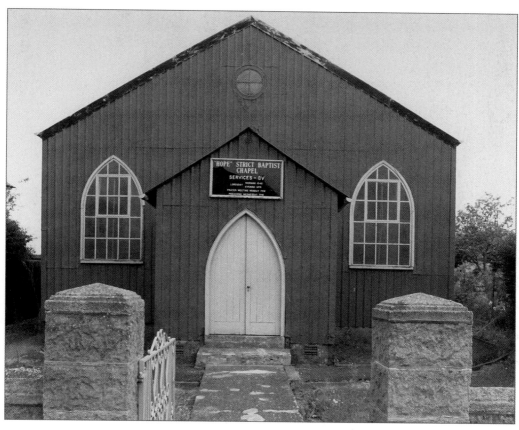

The Strict Baptists' chapel called Hope, in Arcal Street, Sedgley, was a corrugated iron building from 1927 until 1982, and was painted red which eventually faded. The picture below shows its rather light and airy interior. (See also page 73.) *(Both pictures David Field)*

A brand new tin building was provided for the congregation of Birch Coppice Primitive Methodist Chapel, Quarry Bank, in 1888. It was used until 1958 when it was demolished to be replaced with a brick-built chapel. A bus stop outside the present building is still called the Tin Chapel. *(Mary Rousell)*

This building on the corner of Eggington Road, Wollaston, was built in 1926 to house a congregation of Open Brethren who had previously used a gospel hall in Union Street, Stourbridge. It is now called the Wollaston Evangelical Church, and when this picture was taken in 2004 it had just been repainted in a light stone colour, after years of being muddy brown. Choice of colour can transform an iron building. *(NW)*

The opening and dedicating of a new chapel was equally important whether the building was constructed of the best quality bricks or of humble corrugated iron. Here we see a big crowd turn out to see the opening of the Congregational tin chapel in Green Lane, Blackheath, on 21 October 1900. It was built by Eli Hadley & Sons for £400, and the dedication seen here is being carried out by the Revd T.G. Vinson.

The Congregationalists in Green Lane laid the foundation stones of a brick-built church in 1908 and opened it on 1 March 1909. The corrugated iron chapel then became a Sunday School and hall. Several descendants of people seen in this 1918 picture still attend the church, but the tin chapel has now become an Age Concern day centre. *(Both pictures Ivan Williams collection)*

The Good Shepherd Mission at Lyde Green, opened in October 1909, was a good example of tin chapel architecture. It was destroyed by fire in 1958. *(Peter Barnsley collection)*

The little iron chapel in Brades Village, believed to be a mission established by St Michael's in Tividale, photographed in April 1995, was typical of the genre. Painted black but with a red-tiled roof it was almost invisible, and presumably no-one noticed when it disappeared altogether a few years later. *(NW)*

5 Missions & Mission Halls

Strictly speaking, a mission chapel or church is a satellite of an existing church – an 'outreach project' in which a congregation tries to reach those feeling too isolated to attend the existing church. The Church of England found that establishing mission churches was a way of keeping up with the expansion of the nonconformists and could provide a community with a church more quickly than the process of endlessly dividing parishes. However, the nonconformists, particularly the Methodists, also engaged in the practice of building outlying missions. By their nature missions often used rather temporary buildings. The problem, of course, is that the congregation in a mission often became quite independent of the parent church, and in some cases broke away, as in the case of the Waterfall Lane Mission (see page 36).

Mission chapels ought therefore to be distinguished from mission halls, which were usually defiantly independent from the start, even if appearing to be part of a larger denomination. In some cases they were breakaways from existing congregations, in other cases they were established as a result of evangelical crusades or revivals. Often they flourished through the efforts of small committed groups, or even individuals (see page 127: the Fenton Street Mission Hall, Brierley Hill).

The Black Country is full of surviving independent missions, and new ones are still being created – often using an amazing array of secondhand premises.

St Michael's Church in Brierley Hill established this wooden mission church in The Delph in 1886 and it survived until 1952. Although it survived the surrounding mining activity, the building was weakened by wind and eight iron hawsers eventually anchored it to the ground – but it still swayed. It was known as the Church of the Good Shepherd, and like all missions enjoyed quite an independent existence. It is still possible to trace the site of the building when exploring The Delph.

The Pond Lane Mission, Pond Lane, Wolverhampton, is a satellite of St Luke's Church, Blakenhall. It was established in 1896 and is still going strong. Here we see the Thursday afternoon Bible class meeting in the summer of 2004, led by Thelma Hollinshead. *(NW)*

The warm interior of the Pond Lane Mission, June 2004. A Mr Arthur Dodd, many years the Sunday School Superintendent, did much to refurbish the building and at some stage re-clad the exterior. Mr Hinde's skill as a cabinet-maker is reflected in the woodwork around the altar. *(NW)*

Christ Church, Coseley, built three missions, and this one – St Cuthbert's, in Broad Street, Wallbrook, survived until 4 July 2004. Foundation stones were laid on 23 June 1896, and the chapel was opened on 27 October. In the early years it was run by some lay brothers, but from the First World War onwards the Church Army took over. Captain Vivian Budden arrived in 1925 and stayed until 1982! It became an important social centre for the unemployed in the 1920s, as well as providing all the normal activities of chapel life. It survived a couple of demolition threats and enjoyed at least two major refurbishments. *(NW)*

St Cuthbert's Church Army Band, Coseley, in the late 1920s, with Captain Budden seen standing on the left. *(Ray Baggott collection)*

Sunday School anniversaries seem to have been a nonconformist tradition rather than an Anglican one, but mission churches seem to have adopted such practices. (another reason for regarding them as chapels). Captain Buddon and the girls from the Sunday School are seen in this 1950s photograph. The window was later filled in and the chairs were replaced. *(Ray Baggott collection)*

The anniversaries at St Cuthbert's also featured a parade around the streets of Wallbrook. This mid-1960s picture was taken in Rounds Hill Road. *(Ray Baggott collection)*

St Cuthbert's banner comes out for a Sunday School parade in the late 1980s. It is seen in Broad Street, just outside the mission. *(Ray Baggott collection)*

Since the 1980s the congregation at St Cuthbert's has declined, and on 4 July 2004 the mission held its last service. As can be seen here a large congregation filled the mission at that final service, swelled by worshippers from Christ Church. Although fairly high church in form, the service was very 'spirit led' in the style popular in evangelical chapels. Such are the complications of what is 'church' and what is 'chapel'. *(NW)*

The Grange Road Mission

In the area in which the ground falls away from Blackheath down towards Old Hill there were a number of pits with names like The Fly and The Old Lion, as well as Waterfall Lane Colliery and Haden Hill No. 1, all of which were virtually worked out by the turn of the century. St Paul's parish church in Blackheath built a substantial brick mission church in Waterfall Lane to serve this area, and all went well until a new vicar at St Paul's tried to force a high church style of worship upon the mission's congregation. The congregation rebelled and began worshipping in each other's homes until they could find a new place to meet.

A new home was found in an old malthouse on the corner of Tory Street and Waterfall Lane. It was a dilapidated building behind a shop belonging to Mrs. Owen who leased it to the congregation on a temporary basis for a minimal rent. After much cleaning and makeshift repairs the ex-malthouse was ready to become the Tory Street Mission Hall on 15 April 1906: Easter Sunday. In the absence of any pews, everyone had to lend the hall some chairs – with their names chalked on them so that they might be returned as pews were gradually acquired.

There was not much comfort at first, but over the years the walls were clad with matchboarding and the roof was repaired and slightly raised at the same time. A room was added to house the Sunday School. In 1919 an organ was acquired from a church in Quinton, and this Banfield organ of 1865 vintage is still in use today. Pew-making had been the responsibility of one Jim Evans, who in 1912 had also

The Mission Hall, Grange Road, between Old Hill and Blackheath, as it is today. The Waterfall Lane building also survives as a bedding warehouse. The banner is illustrated on page 21. *(NW)*

Hazel Plant, Marjorie Breakwell, Cliff and Beryl Davison and Karen Thornton at the Grange Road Mission Hall, 6 June 2004. *(NW)*

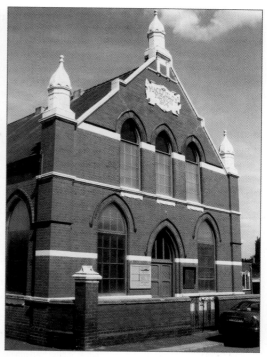

At the other end of Old Hill is a mission hall as opposed to a mission – as explained on page 31. Here we find the Macefield Mission, in Claremont Street, photographed in its centenary year – 2004. The hall has been linked, via the Wesleyan Reform Union, with Campbell Street in Brockmoor and the Bethel in Willenhall Road, Wolverhampton, but the most striking thing about such missions is their independence. *(NW)*

acquired the old Waterfall Lane Sunday School banner for £20. This beautiful George Tuthill banner also survives in the Mission Hall today, along with some of the reversible pews.

In the 1930s the old Tory Street was demolished to be replaced with Grange Road, and the mission changed its name. Since that time perhaps very little has changed apart from the gradual decline in the size of the congregation. Today's superintendent is Cliff Davison, but he is only the fourth person to be in that post. He took over from Bill Finch, who in turn had taken over from Horace Plant. Horace's daughter, Hazel, is still the mission's treasurer. Horace had taken over from Sam Parkes – a crane driver at the Coombs Wood Works, whose life was totally devoted to the mission. Cliff's wife, Beryl, who has attended the mission since the age of 4, has memories stretching back to Sam Parkes – whose picture still hangs in the Sunday School room. The Davisons describe themselves as independent low church Anglicans, but perhaps it is the word independent that defines the spirit that has ensured such continuity within this little mission hall.

The simple, but elegant, interior of the Macefield Mission Hall in Claremont Street, Old Hill, as it is today. *(John James)*

Macefield Mission officials photographed while attending a centenary pig-roast, 10 July 2004. Back row, left to right: Gerald Carpenter, Ivan Rudge, Valerie Hill, John Ruston. Front row: Irene Ruston, Kathleen Woodhall, Edith Edgar, Stan Bealey, Iris Whitall, Ron Whitall. (Iris was involved with the Boys' Brigade at the Mission for forty-seven years until forced to retire at the age of 70.) *(John James)*

6 The North-East Frontier

Essington's Chapel at Allens Rough

If anyone doubts Essington's credentials regarding its association with the Black Country, they only have to think about geology and in particular coal. The northern boundary of the Black Country coalfield was the Bentley Fault, and along this line a number of villages and communities developed and prospered with the coming and going of the pits. A reminder of this is the font to be found in Essington's Chapel. Designed by Essington's late historian and champion, Jim Evans, it takes the form of a miner's safety lamp.

Although John Wesley visited Hilton Hall, home of the Vernon family, the local coalowners, in 1785 and 1787, it is the footsteps of Hugh Bourne that seem to have been more significant. Hugh Bourne was one of the founders of Primitive Methodism, and he walked the 34 miles from Tunstall, where the sect had begun, to Essington in April 1810. Early enthusiasm for Primitive Methodism seems to have waned only to be recharged in the second half of the century with renewed mining activity and an influx of colliers from Shropshire and other parts of the Black Country. A chapel was built at Newtown on the main road from Walsall to Cannock in 1865, followed by another at Essington Wood in 1872.

At the beginning of the twentieth Century the folks in Essington purchased some land just outside the parish from the Ashmore Park Colliery Company at a cost of

The red brick chapel at Allens Rough, Essington, of 1906, and the blue-painted wooden Sunday School building opened on 16 April 1955, photographed in May 2004. The front elevation of the chapel has lost some elegance as a result of filling in the main window. Proposals regarding putting a commemorative window back have been shelved pending likely closure. *(NW)*

Essington's font, in the shape of a miner's lamp, was designed by Jim Evans as part of the refurbishment of the chapel, completed in September 1962. *(NW)*

£30. This area is known as Allens Rough. Fund raising then began and it was not until 1906 that funds were sufficient to build a chapel, the foundation stone being laid on 30 July 1906. The architect was T. Saunders and the builders were J & F Wooton of Bloxwich. It was completed in time for the official opening on 15 November 1906.

Although built in a rather remote location, the little chapel at Allens Rough was always a busy place. Like other chapels its history consists of a never-ending tale of improvements and additions – ranging from installation of gas lighting in 1915 and then electric lighting in 1934 to the grand organ installation of 1923. There was a thriving Sunday School, and groups like the Women's Liberals and the Rechabites all used the facilities at Allens Rough. The adjoining wooden building was opened as Sunday School and Youth Centre in 1955. The chapel enjoyed a major refurbishment in the early 1960s when the font in the shape of a miner's lamp was added.

In recent times modern housing has been built on the chapel's doorstep and it is no longer so isolated, but ironically this seems to have hardly added to the congregation at all. As the chapel approaches its centenary there is talk of closure in the air.

A Sunday School anniversary at Allens Rough, 1950s. The older girls are even wearing white gloves for the occasion. Messrs Hawkins of Walsall built the organ in 1923, resulting in some rebuilding of the interior. *(Marlene Evans collection)*

The Short Heath Methodists

Where else might one expect to find a Methodist chapel other than on the corner of Wesley Road? In this case the Wesley Road is in Short Heath in the north-eastern corner of the Black Country, and it is a chapel whose history has been carefully recorded and archived over the years.

Coal was mined in this area north of Willenhall, and it seems that a collier took the initiative to start Methodist meetings back in the 1820s. A small chapel was built in Coltham Road in 1826 and seven years later was replaced with a larger building, which was also used as a Sunday School and day school. (In fact it was used as a day school until replaced by the school at New Invention in 1908, and both Coltham Road buildings survived until 1971.)

The church hiding behind the trees on the corner of Wesley Road today was built in the 1880s. Foundation stones were laid with great ceremony on 13 July 1881 and the chapel was opened on 11 April 1882. It was designed by B. Baker and built by Thomas Tildesley – both of Willenhall. It was of the Gothic style popular at the time, looking far more church-like than chapel-like, which is quite interesting in the light of its proximity to the parish church.

The history of the chapel has been put into print on several occasions – for example at the centenary in 1981 and on a Local History Society card in 2001. It is a story of continual renewal and development, both inside the chapel and in the facilities provided around it. Thus the chapel combines features of recent modernisations with a wealth of historical detail from the past.

The Short Heath Methodists football team was known as The Cobblers because it was managed by Fred Onions (1908–94), local youth leader, preacher, councillor – and local cobbler. Short Heath seems to have produced its fair share of dedicated Methodists and local characters – often one and the same thing. Fred Onions was a good example. His tiny cobbler's shop in the front room of 81 Coltham Road was where he 'repaired soles' and 'refurbished souls'. In 1992 he celebrated sixty years as a local preacher in a ceremony shared with Bill Poole. Today 95-year-old Bill Poole made all the chapel's archives available to the author of this book, determined that Short Heath be put on the map! At the age of 91 he retired as Short Heath's organist after seventy-seven years – having started at the keyboard of a harmonium – but his memories embrace the Sunday School, the Wesley Guild, and the chapel's tennis courts where he and his wife Joan, from Lane Head Methodists, had often played.

Victorian engraving of Short Heath Methodist Chapel – a view now obscured by trees.
(*Chapel Archives*)

The interior at Short Heath as re-consecrated on 28 August 1952. Like many Methodist chapels, it once had an inscription written above the arch in Gothic script. This one read 'Enter into His gates with thanksgiving'. The pulpit was originally beneath the centre of this arch. *(Short Heath archives)*

This view, from the gallery, was taken during the 1975 150th Sunday School Anniversary service. Note the pews are now divided to create a central aisle. A new commemorative window has appeared behind the altar. *(Short Heath archives)*

The stone-laying party assembled on 28 June 1958 at the side of Short Heath Methodist Chapel, with the minister, the Revd A. Kinsey. The foundation stone had just been laid for the Wesley Hall which was about to be built to replace the Sunday School building – the 'Mark 2' chapel building in Coltham Road. Fred Onions is second left. *(Short Heath archives)*

Personalities have always been important at Short Heath. This picture was taken in June 1992 when Bill Poole (left) and Fred Onions (right) were both 83 and both celebrating sixty years of preaching. When Bill retired from the post of organist at the age of 91, he had been playing at the organ keys for seventy-seven years. Fred had been a well-known figure in Short Heath, as youth leader, football team manager, local councillor on Willenhall Urban District Council and famous cobbler of Coltham Road. *(Short Heath archives)*

The Primitive Methodists built their first chapel in New Invention in 1851, but replaced it with this building, on the opposite side of the Lichfield Road, in 1898 at a time when New Invention was beginning to grow into a more substantial community. *(NW)*

The Primitive Methodists built this little chapel in Spring Bank on the north-eastern frontiers of Willenhall in 1879. It closed in 1974 when an aging and declining congregation was faced with heavy repair bills. Eventually the building was sold to the Church of God of Prophecy, but they too declined and joined a church in Bilston! The Revd Gilmore Grant came to the building in about 2002 and runs it as the Light House Christian Centre, which met previously in several venues in Willenhall. Things now seem to be improving and links have been established with the community and other churches. *(NW)*

7 Willenhall & Darlaston

Willenhall and Darlaston were once heavily industrialised urban districts, each with plenty of chapels. Darlaston played a key part in bringing Primitive Methodism to the Black Country, and was the scene of an interesting moment in John Wesley's travels in 1743: local magistrates failed to respond when the mob tried to drag him before them. Wesley was ducked in the Tame before being released.

In Willenhall the nonconformist cause seems to have been helped by the lifestyle adopted by the incumbent at St Giles' from 1788 to 1834. William Moreton was an intemperate supporter of cock-fighting and bull-baiting. His disillusioned flock provided ready converts to Methodism. By the 1880s there were six Wesleyan chapels in the Willenhall circuit, Union Street, Walsall Road, Portobello, Monmer Lane, Short Heath and March End. The Primitive Methodists were represented in Russell Street, Lane Head, New Invention, Spring Bank and Portobello. The New Connexion provided chapels in Froysell Street and Portobello. (Portobello was well served with Methodist chapels!) Added to these were several Baptist chapels.

The picture was similar in Darlaston. George Philpott, a steward at Darlaston Green, wrote to the *Black Country Bugle* a few years ago to confess, 'At one time I could stand on the steps of one chapel in Darlaston, throw a brick in any direction, and almost be sure to break a window in another!' He recalled the chapels at Pinfold Street, Great Croft Street, Joynson Street, Old Park Road (Kings Hill), Bell Street, Fallings Heath and Darlaston Green.

Willenhall's first Wesleyan chapel was built in about 1810. A quarter of a century later the congregation had outgrown this chapel and a new one was under construction at the junction of Union Street and Upper Lichfield Street: it opened in October 1837. The building seen here was the result of rebuilding in the 1860s. Opening on 5 July 1864, it was built by Job Wilkes and designed by Edward Banks who also designed Wolverhampton's High Level station. It became Trinity after amalgamation with Russell Street and Walsall Road in 1965, but closed in 1996. Note the railings on the left are in front of the Lichfield Street Baptist chapel – see next page. (NW)

The Baptist cause was represented in the Little London quarter of Willenhall from the 1780s onwards, at one stage much influenced by the Baptists at Darkhouse, Coseley. The first chapel opened in 1811, but the building seen here was opened on 15 June 1851, followed by a public tea meeting in the schoolroom. The frontage originally featured a triangular pediment, but this was removed in 1970. The chapel survived to celebrate its 200th birthday but closed in 1994. It is now used by an Apostolic congregation and bears the name Mount Olive. *(NW)*

The Baptist chapel in Lichfield Street, Willenhall, was formed by a breakaway group from Little London. It was built in 1862, the foundation stone being laid on 5 May of that year, and was known as Mount Calvary Baptist Church. The Baptists ceased using it in 1976. The New Testament Church now meets here. *(NW)*

The original congregation of Providence Chapel, New Road, Willenhall, was formed in about 1829 as a result of the preaching of the Rowley Regis pastor, Daniel Matthews (see below). The building seen here was built in 1879 – giving Willenhall three Baptist churches in fairly close proximity. The current Baptist congregation now meets in the rear of the building, and since March 2004 the Restoration Bible Church has used the main chapel. *(NW)*

Debra Wiley, a minister from the USA, preaches to the Restoration Bible Church congregation in the Willenhall Providence Chapel in 2004. Behind her is the memorial to Daniel Matthews who had preached at Rowley Regis from 1829 and then at Willenhall from 1841 until his death in 1881. *(Pastor Lloyd Abel collection)*

A Wesleyan chapel was built at Darlaston Green in 1844 but collapsed as a result of mining in 1869. This building, the replacement, was built in 1870–1. To the left was the wooden schoolroom, demolished in 1948, known as The Matchbox. The chapel survived to celebrate its centenary in 1970, but closed a year later. *(George Phillpott)*

At Darlaston Green the Ladies Effort of 1930 was just what it claimed to be – even the minister in the centre of the picture is really one of the ladies! *(George Phillpott)*

8   Wolverhampton

Wolverhampton's chapels will have to be dealt with more comprehensively in a further volume. The history of the town's chapels reflects its general history of outward expansion, growing into the city that is now surrounded by miles of suburbia. For example, both the Baptists and Congregationalists built large chapels in the town centre and then nurtured new chapels in suburbia – the latter having survived and the former now demolished! (Even the Church of England's churches have survived in the suburbs while those nearer the town centre have vanished, as if to underline this pattern.)

Wolverhampton has always enjoyed a slightly more diverse population than its Black Country neighbours, so we should not be surprised that one of the most chapel-like survivors in the city centre is in fact an ex-Jewish synagogue, now used by an unreformed group of traditional Anglicans. Added to that are chapels/churches provided for Italian, Polish, Ukrainian, Punjabi and Welsh-speaking congregations.

In this chapter we will look at a couple of examples of town-centre congregations spawning congregations in the suburbs (one Congregational, the other Baptist), as well as the Bethel Chapel on the Willenhall Road, and All Saints in Parkfield.

The Revd S.C. Cook lays the foundation stone of the Staveley Road Baptist chapel, or Tabernacle, on 12 September 1931, assisted by Mr Tomlinson, the architect. In the left foreground are Walter Eveson in the school cap and Ted Smith in the flat cap. Ted is still a member of the congregation in 2004. *(Tabernacle archives)*

The large Baptist chapel in Waterloo Road, Wolverhampton, is representative of a number of large city-centre chapels that have been demolished. This chapel was built in 1863 and survived long enough to enjoy a centenary, but closed in 1969 and was demolished in 1970. Its congregation, of Particular Baptists, had been able to trace roots going back to 1830 when a building had been provided in Cannon Street, then moving to St James Street before coming to Waterloo Road. *(Express & Star)*

Below: Most Wulfrunians will remember the Congregational Chapel on the corner of Queen Street, in the town centre, and another on Snow Hill. Both could trace their ancestry back to the earliest days of dissent in Wolverhampton, and both subsequently planted congregations in the suburbs – where we would find them today. A Stafford Street Mission was established in 1877 and the chapel on the right was built in 1886, with the school on the left added in about 1910. This picture was taken in 1936, when the congregation was celebrating its fiftieth birthday. The buildings have not survived, but at one time were home to Wolverhampton's Maternity and Child Welfare Department. *(Express & Star)*

The exterior and interior of the Tabernacle Baptist Chapel, Dunstall Road, Wolverhampton, photographed in 2004 just as restoration work had begun on the chapel's raked floor. It was opened in the summer of 1932. A two manual pipe organ was installed soon after, and for sixty years occupied the space between the two windows. *(NW)*

The Congregationalists in Queen Street, in the centre of Wolverhampton, promoted a number of missions to the suburbs and beyond. On 2 February 1905 they laid the foundation stone at Lea Road in Penn Fields, and on 2 July Alderman Baldwin Bantock opened the chapel/school building seen above. Immediately 130 scholars were enrolled and 35 members of the Queen Street congregation were 'dismissed' to join the newcomers at Penn Fields. On 7 March 1932 the chapel, seen below, was opened to serve the much enlarged congregation. *(Barbara Prettie and John Hughes)*

Looking towards the back of the 1932 building at Lea Road Congregational Chapel, showing the organ, which has been transferred and modified for use in the present building. The last service was held here in 1994 and the congregation moved into the 1905 building (with 1960s additions) and suffered leaks and privations until their brand new church was ready for opening on 24 February 1996. *(John Lloyd)*

Lea Road had been the first all-electric chapel in Wolverhampton, and prides itself in being home to the first Age Concern Day Centre and the first Mencap playgroup. For years the Saints Youth Club was so popular it virtually wore out the old 1905 building! Here we look towards the front of the 1932 building at Christmas 1993. *(Barbara Prettie)*

The Lea Road United Reformed Church, as it is now, was built in the early 1990s to replace the 1905 and 1932 buildings. The octagonal building was designed by Brian Jeffries and built by A.M. Griffiths, and was opened on 24 February 1996. It is a busy lively centre within the community of Penn Fields. The Asian Calvary church also holds regular worship in Punjabi and Hindi in this building. *(NW)*

In 2004 the Bethel Chapel on Willenhall Road, Wolverhampton, provides a striking visual contrast to Lea Road's modern octagon. The Bethel congregation was formed in the 1870s, led by John Colbourne, and first rented a stable in a coal yard. With some generous assistance from Sir Alfred Hickman the little chapel was built; it opened on 2 August 1890, and became part of the Wesleyan Reform Union. *(NW)*

On 5 May 1990 the congregation at the Bethel Chapel, Willenhall Road, celebrated their centenary with a Victorian evening. Pastor George Jones is in the pulpit and present leader John Griffiths is on the right. *(Kathleen Rogers)*

The 14th Wolverhampton Boys' Brigade Company was based at the Bethel Chapel, led for many years by Alfred Drew. Mr Harold Hunt of the nearby Chillington Ironworks sits in the centre of this company portrait, with Mr Drew on his right and a Mr Colbourne, son of one of the founders of the Bethel, on his left. *(Mrs L. Evans)*

Parkfield Road Primitive Methodist Chapel was opened in 1875, and two rows of neighbouring terraced housing were called Clowes Terrace and Hugh Bourne Terrace in memory of the founders of Primitive Methodism. Community facilities were added at the rear of the chapel in 1957 reflecting the success of its Sunday School and youth work, but eventually the congregation declined and it closed as a Methodist chapel in 1991. It is now known as All Saints' Church and is part of the Bethel United Apostolic Church of Jesus Christ which has its headquarters at Kelvin Way, West Bromwich. Here, elders and choir lead the packed congregation at All Saints', Parkfield Road, on 18 July 2004 at a service where some of the children are about to be blessed. A good example of a chapel where the pews are full! *(NW)*

9   Bilston

Iron-mad Wilkinson established his iron works in Bradley in the mid-eighteenth century and began to change the Black Country from a local producer of coal and iron on a modest scale into a mighty producer of these commodities on the national and international scene. Henry Newbolt, born in Bilston in 1862, described the consequences as 'a wilderness of man's own making'.

John Wesley visited the future wilderness in 1745 and in the late 1760s when a minister in the Staffordshire Circuit, by which time local Methodist Societies had formed. As in the other Black Country communities in which industrialisation was underway he met the fury of the mob, and at the same time made many converts. Another visitor to Bilston, in the nineteenth century, was cholera. During the 1832 outbreak the Methodists made a name for themselves in fearlessly dealing with it. During the second outbreak, of 1849, there was a broader response and even the future Cardinal Newman, then a local assistant priest, joined those dealing with the epidemic.

One should not be surprised to find there has been a plethora of chapels built in the Bilston area, some of which have disappeared. Much has been recorded of how they have coped with two hundred and fifty years of continually changing circumstances. There is only space here to cover a fraction of the subject.

Methodism was established in Bilston during John Wesley's lifetime, and the first chapel in the area was in Temple Street, Loxdale. The site in Swan Bank, close to the centre of Bilston, has been associated with Methodism since 1823, and the Wesleyan chapel here was rebuilt on several occasions. The huge building seen here was completed in 1890 and opened on 12 January 1891. To the left is the Manse, and the campus included a Sunday School and burial ground. This building was demolished in 1969 reflecting the changes of that time. *(Harold & Iris Dale)*

The Revd Brian O'Gorman, President of the Methodist Conference, lays the foundation stone at Swan Bank on 12 July 1969. In 1963 the Wesleyan Society at Swan Bank amalgamated with the Primitive Methodists in the High Street, and 1969 marked the building of this new Bilston Methodist Church. Since that date the congregations from Bunkers Hill (Cold Lanes), Ladymoor, and the Temple Street Mission have also come to Swan Bank. *(Harold & Iris Dale)*

The Swan Bank site today. The new Bilston Methodist Church is on the right – opened on 25 June 1970. The Revd Brian Gorman, who had laid the foundation stone in 1969, returned to open the church as the last event of his Presidency of the Methodist Conference. On the left is the old Sunday School building of 1896 running parallel to Lewis Street. The original chapel and manse (page 57) occupied the foreground facing Bridge Street. *(NW)*

A Swan Bank Sunday School parade on the streets of Bilston, 1980s. The banner on the left is still to be found at Swan Bank, and features the shell symbol found on many Methodist banners on an attractive blue background. *(Harold Dale)*

On 23 June 2002 the scouts at Swan Bank celebrated their twenty-fifth anniversary and joined forces with the Sunday School's anniversary of that year. *(NW)*

The first Primitive Methodist chapel in Bilston was opened in 1825, and was visited by Hugh Bourne on its first anniversary. Its successor was built in the High Street and opened in 1841. It closed at the end of 1961 when the congregation amalgamated with the Methodists at Swan Bank. This 1940s picture was one of several such photos taken by the minister, the Revd W.H. Collins. His son, Harry Collins, still plays the organ at Swan Bank. *(The Revd W.H. Collins)*

The Colds Lane Chapel, Bunkers Hill, seen here in the 1940s, was established as a Primitive Methodist mission from the chapel in the High Street. The mission outlasted the mother-chapel, but amalgamated with Bilston Methodist Church (Swan Bank) in 1966. *(The Revd W.H. Collins)*

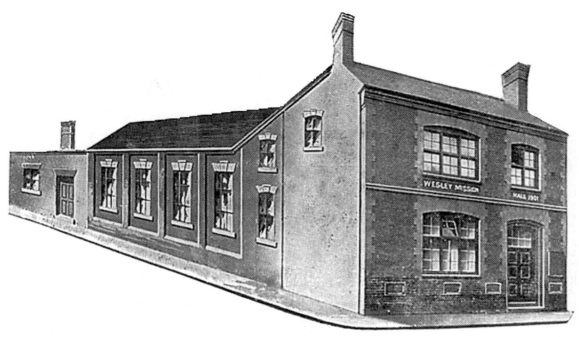

The first Wesleyan Methodist Chapel in Bilston had been in Temple Street, but the congregation moved to Swan Bank in 1823. However, Methodism returned to Temple Street in 1883 when a mission hall was established in a former public house. It was rebuilt in the form seen here in 1901 and accommodated a large Sunday School, Band of Hope and a host of weekday activities. By the time it was celebrating its fiftieth birthday in 1951 the future seemed uncertain, and it eventually merged with the Bilston Methodist Church (Swan Bank). *(Harold & Iris Dale collection)*

The striking white exterior of Ashley's Chapel in Chapel Street, Bilston, 2004. This Congregational Mission was apparently opened by one of the Mander family on 25 October 1870. A stone records that it was built by R. Hickman and designed by G. Bidlake. *(NW)*

Salop Street Primitive Methodist Chapel, in Bradley, probably dated from 1846. It closed in about 1959 with the amalgamation of Methodist chapels in Bradley. *(The Revd W.H. Collins)*

To the west of Bilston are a number of villages linked to it. Bradley is famous as the spot chosen by Wilkinson for his ironworks. The local Wesleyan Methodists persuaded him to provide a cast iron chapel, of which the cast iron pulpit survives. The chapel, in Hall Green Street, was replaced in 1835 and again in 1900 and 1980. The Primitive Methodists built three chapels – Salop Street (see previous page), Lower Bradley and this one at Daisy Bank. The 'Prims' were well supported among the iron-workers and rolling mill hands of the district. The building, seen here in the 1940s, was erected in 1892, replacing one affected by subsidence. *(The Revd W.H. Collins)*

Priestfield supported a small Primitive Methodist chapel in Ward Street until 1965 when its congregation gave up and joined their larger neighbour in George Street (see next page). The £1,000 gained from the sale of the Ward Street chapel helped pay for the renovation of George Street! The chapel was built on land between two railway lines – which met at the junction at Priestfield – and passing trains loosened the slates on the roof and drowned the sermons. A leaking roof, gaslight and a hand-pumped organ did nothing to inhibit the pride of the folks of Priestfield, and its anniversaries are remembered with great fondness. *(The Revd W.H. Collins)*

10 Hell Lane to Sodom
& Up the Bonk

Between Bilston and Sedgley lay a number of villages now obscured by modern roads, endless housing development and local government boundaries. This takes us through Ettingshall, Lanesfield, Deepfields, and up the eastern flank of Sedgley Beacon to Hurst Hill, where we can turn right to Cinder Hill or left to Coppice.

In the nineteenth century Ettingshall Lane was known as Hell Lane, but a small Methodist Society built a chapel there which seems to have opened in 1806. It was replaced in 1830 but the new building was affected by subsidence and a third chapel was built on land between George Street and John Street in 1842. Once again mining took its toll and a fourth building had to be built in the 1880s facing George Street, opening on 12 February 1883. This 2004 picture shows the 1880s building with a single door porch that was added in about 1950. *(NW)*

The Methodists used George Street until 1988. It was reopened by the Full Gospel African Methodist Episcopal Zion Church in May 1992. Some of the present congregation is seen here in July 2004. *(NW)*

The Sodom Primitive Methodist Chapel at Upper Ettingshall was first built in 1826, but the building still in use today dates back to 1850. One historian has pointed out that of the twelve original trustees only three could sign their name. The rather stark cream exterior, seen above in 2004, gives little indication of the delightful interior – as seen on the opposite page. *(NW)*

Organist Helen Emery and choirmistress Pam Hughes prepare for the Sunday School anniversary at Upper Ettingshall on 16 May 2004. *(NW)*

Girls outnumber the boys at the Upper Ettingshall Sunday School Anniversary of 1933, with pupils on a tiered platform built up from the ground floor, surrounding the pulpit and almost reaching the balcony! *(Jennifer Hill)*

At the Sunday School Anniversary of 2004 a few children take part from the front row of the choir stalls just in front of the organ. The preacher, Geoff Allman, is rather isolated in the pulpit below. *(NW)*

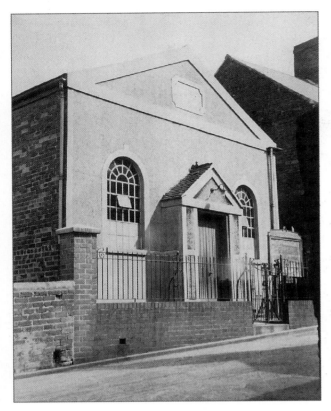

Cinder Hill, sometimes spelt as one word, is the sort of place that you might miss if you blinked. The hamlet nestles on the flank of Sedgley Beacon. Its tiny chapel was built by the Primitive Methodists in the middle of the nineteenth century and probably opened in 1851. A stone was laid on 28 July 1951 to celebrate its centenary, but 1 January 1852 is also sometimes quoted as the opening date. The chapel closed in 2000 and has been demolished. *(The Revd W.H. Collins)*

The congregation at Cinder Hill was photographed in the chapel just before its closure. Back row, left to right: Sid Cole, Edna Beasley, the Revd John Barrett, Frank Jones. Front row: Margaret Webb, Joyce Williams, Muriel Richards, Dorothy Brookes, Kit Jones, Barbara Watkins. *(John Hughes)*

Coppice Baptist Chapel was built in 1804, and this photograph was taken in its bicentenary year! It is a listed building and is one of the oldest local places of worship to survive into the twenty-first century so well preserved and in its original state. The rear extension was added in 1875. *(NW)*

In the nineteenth century the area we now call Hurst Hill was called Can Lane. The first Wesleyan chapel in Can Lane was built on the opposite side of the road to the present building and dates back to 1798. The present building was built in 1864 in the classical style popular in the mid-nineteenth century. A Sunday School building was added, and then a hall. *(NW)*

The Hurst Hill Methodists' Sunday School anniversary of 30 June 2002 also celebrated two hundred years of Sunday School at Hurst Hill. In the centre is Pam Hughes, anniversary organiser, and in the pulpit are Graham Hancox, organist, and guest preacher the Revd John Sadler. *(NW)*

The 2004 Anniversary at Hurst Hill was a two-day event, with the traditional service on Sunday. Saturday afternoon on 26 June, seen here, was spent re-creating an end of Second World War 'street party' in the safety of the Sunday School hall. Red, white and blue flags also decorated the chapel for the anniversary service. *(NW)*

11 Through the Villages

As we have seen, by making our way from Bilston, out through Ettingshall and up the slopes of Sedgley Beacon, it is still possible to encounter the Black Country as a string of villages. This can be replicated by a journey from Coseley to Woodsetton and up to Sedgley itself, along the ridge and down in Lower Gornal and Gornal Wood. Once again there are a variety of Methodist and Baptist chapels along the route.

The journey can begin at the Old Meeting House, Old Meeting Road, Coseley. A congregation was established in this area by the Revd Joseph Eccleshall in 1662, when thrown out of his job at the parish church in Sedgley for refusing to sign the Act of Conformity. It became a Unitarian congregation and eventually became the richest congregation in Coseley. A Sunday School building was added to the original meeting house, and in 1874 the very church-like building was erected in Old Meeting Road. Today it seems to have fallen on hard times and the congregation has evaporated, but it has been a small congregation long enough to grow used to the idea. The regulars have been attending all their lives and wouldn't dream of going elsewhere.

The Baptists have also been in Coseley for a long time. Their Ebenezer chapel now forms a landmark on the Birmingham–Wolverhampton New Road. It seceded from Providence in 1856 and the chapel was built in 1858 in the Classical style.

The small congregation of the Old Meeting House at the 2004 Anniversary, 4 July, turned out to listen to Tom Marriott, President of the Midland Union of Unitarians, address them on humility. The best view of the interior is seen here from beside the altar, looking towards the gallery and the organ. *(NW)*

The original Coseley Unitarian Meeting House was probably to the right of this picture, and the present Sunday School building on the right was the second chapel. The very church-like building in the Gothic style of the period was added in 1874, the foundation stone being laid on 16 November. The congregation now meets fortnightly but seems determined to continue. *(NW)*

Mr Whiteman at the Old Meeting House, Coseley, in May 1951, flanked on the left by the retiring May Queen, Pat Webb, and on the right by the new May Queen, Beryl Parkes. *(Beryl Cattell collection)*

The Ebenezer Baptist Chapel in Coseley found itself occupying a very public location as a result of the building of the Wolverhampton to Birmingham New Road in 1927. It began life in 1856 as a Particular Baptist succession from Coseley's Providence Chapel. By September 1858 the congregation had managed to build this chapel in fine Classical style. *(NW)*

Mount Tabor, Tipton Road, Woodsetton, was built by a Methodist New Connexion congregation in 1859 and closed in 1999. Although very small and intimate, the chapel was packed on a couple of recent occasions when the Black Country Society held its annual Christmas Carol Service there. Note the war memorial on the left. *(NW)*

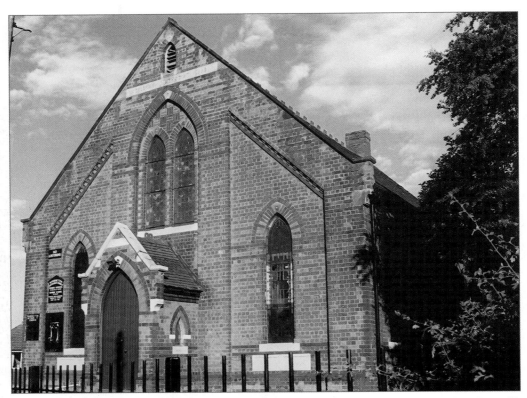

Woodsetton Methodist Church, off Parkes Hall Road, and known locally as 'Under the Hill', was built in 1882 by a Wesleyan congregation that had been meeting since 1810. The chapel and adjoining schoolroom was designed by Charles Round, of Tipton and built by Jones & Son of Sedgley. It opened on 5 December 1882. *(NW)*

Even a tiny chapel like Mount Tabor could mount a sizeable Sunday School Anniversary, as seen in this 1949 photograph. *(Margaret Webb)*

Approaching Sedgley from Woodsetton one comes across this chapel in Tipton Street. The first Primitive Methodist chapel to open in Sedgley was in Gospel End Street in 1821. By the 1850s the Society was hoping to build larger premises where there would be space to build a schoolroom. The result was this chapel, which opened in November 1857, followed by the schoolroom of 1881. The congregation now meets in the schoolroom and a question mark has hung over the future of the building for some time. Local interest in the building has led to its listing. Seen here in 2004, it awaits a sympathetic developer. *(NW)*

The Hope Strict Baptist Chapel in Arcal Street was first built as a tin tabernacle in 1927 for a congregation led by Joseph Field until 1939 (see page 27). His son, Joseph Edward Field, took over for the next forty years. Since then it has been led by the Revd Mr Oakley, and this new chapel was built in 1982 by Messrs Stocks of Leeds. *(NW)*

The little wooden chapel used by the Strict Baptists at Moden Hill is a perfect example of the modest chapel. Its congregation formed in the 1920s as a breakaway from the Robert Street Baptists of Gornal, and it maintains its independence to this day. Moden Hill, Hope and Rehoboth (Jews Lane) all seem to have been products of succession from Robert Street Baptist Chapel (Providence). *(NW)*

Because of their architectural modesty, small chapels and their interiors do not seem to have been frequently photographed. However, they are often warm intimate buildings strongly contrasting with the cold stony interiors of the large Gothic churches. The interior of Moden Hill Baptist Chapel is a good example. (Compare with Hope in Arcal Street – both in tin tabernacle days and today, or with places like Lodge Farm and the Grange Road Mission, Old Hill.) *(NW)*

The turnpike road from Sedgley to Dudley passes Upper Gornal where Methodist chapels have amalgamated and been provided with a modern church, but the back road descends to Lower Gornal via Ruiton and Five Ways. The Independent Congregational Church at Ruiton has a history stretching back to the 1770s. A major restoration marked its bicentenary. Look for the elaborate headstones of the Ruiton salt-sellers in its graveyard. *(NW)*

Four chapels exist in close proximity in the area where Robert Street reaches the Five Ways. In Robert Street itself is this building – the Providence Baptist Chapel. Particular Baptists from Turner Street, Lower Gornal, built this imposing chapel designed by George Bidlake. It was opened on 4 October 1874. It suffered five successions during the 1920s and almost closed in 1970, but then enjoyed a revival. *(NW)*

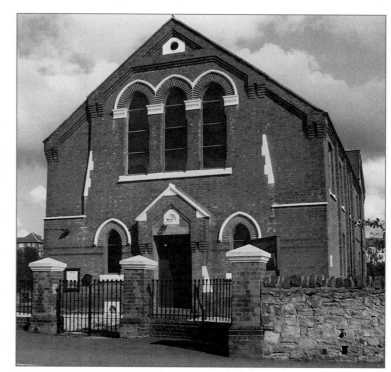

The descent into Gornal Wood is rewarded by the sight of the Zoar Chapel with its rich red brick and stone-coloured terracotta exterior, dominating the centre of the village. The chapel, the third on the site, was built for a Methodist New Connexion congregation in 1906, replacing an 1854 building. The architect was P.H.A. Bailey and the builder was Mark Round of Dudley. The clock was added to the tower in 1919 as a war memorial. *(NW)*

As might be expected by its exterior, the interior of the Zoar Chapel is large and impressive – as seen here, in 2004, from the gallery. *(NW)*

12   Tipton

There is a huge area in the centre of the Black Country where boundaries are difficult to define. The Black Country Development Corporation, created in the mid-1980s to regenerate this area, had a boundary that crossed all previously known boundaries, and set out to unify the area by building its famous Spine Road. The latter offers new Black Country vistas on a route that runs from Moxley to Wednesbury, round to Great Bridge and over to West Bromwich. From your car window it is as difficult to spot a chapel as it is to spot a steelworks, but it was not always so.

In 1965 four Methodist circuits combined to create a new Tipton Circuit, which brought together twenty chapels. The geography is mind-boggling as one takes in their names: Lea Brook, Ocker Hill, Wesley Place, Aston Place (Toll End), New Road, Gospel Oak, Summer Hill, High Street, Regent Street, Trinity, Horseley Heath, St Paul's, Dudley Port, Canal Street, Park Lane, The Park, Bell Street, Bloomfield, Woodsetton and Roseville. Add a few independent chapels to be found in this area and the complexity of the picture is soon overwhelming.

Amalgamations and closures have simplified matters, and in this chapter we pause to take in a few samples of the chapel life of this area.

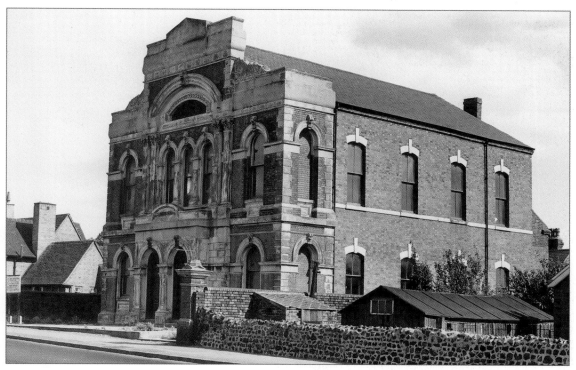

It is difficult to imagine that chapels as vast and as solid as the Wesleyan chapel at Gospel Oak have vanished, but the last service was held on 31 March 1987 and the building was demolished two months later. It was built in 1876, replacing an earlier structure, and held over five hundred worshippers. *(Alan Price)*

A Sunday School parade, led by the band, pauses outside the Sunday School building in Lea Brook, *c*. 1910. The Sunday School building was built in 1902, and the original chapel can be seen in the background. The latter was demolished in 1937. Beyond the chapel it is just possible to make out the outline of the Patent Shaft Steelworks. *(Bob Cooper)*

The Primitive Methodists established themselves at Lea Brook in 1848 and built the chapel seen in the top picture in 1850. When that was demolished in 1937 the congregation moved into the Sunday School building built in 1902, seen here in 2004. *(NW)*

A Sunday School anniversary photograph at Lea Brook Chapel, taken in 1947 and used in the chapel's 'Centenary Celebrations' brochure produced the following year. *(Bob Cooper collection)*

Tipton's 'cathedral' was the Wesleyan chapel built in Park Lane in 1866 by Messrs Trow of Wednesbury. The architect was George Bidlake of Wolverhampton and this is his drawing of the building. A Wesleyan Society had been meeting on this site since John Wesley's own lifetime and a 1750 meeting house was given to Wesley, who in turn passed it on to local trustees. It was demolished to make way for a replacement in 1809. The latter eventually suffered the effects of mining, and this third chapel was opened on 21 September 1866. Today a fourth building occupies the site, built in 1978. *(Keith Hodgkins)*

The little chapel in Wesley Place, Toll End, was founded by Samuel and Mary Oliver, and their grandson, David Oliver, is seen here in 2004 standing in front of the abandoned building. It closed in the late 1970s when replaced with a new building in Bourne Street. *(NW)*

A Methodist New Connexion congregation formed in the 'Puppy Green' area of Tipton in the 1860s and built the chapel in Victoria Road in 1903, opening on 20 June in that year. This building was intended to be the Sunday School, but had to double as both school and chapel. Park Methodist Church is known locally as the 'Little Chapel'. *(NW)*

The choir at the Primitive Methodist Centenary Chapel, Horseley Heath, 1920s. The congregation first met in a chapel in Railway Street, built in 1859 and later sold to be reborn as the Victoria Cinema. The replacement, seen here, was opened in 1907, and was known to most people as the 'Rhubarb Chapel'. *(Alfred Perks)*

The 'Rhubarb Chapel', or Centenary Methodist Chapel, Horseley Heath, closed on 11 March 2004, this picture being taken at the last regular Sunday service on 7 March. *(Keith Hodgkins)*

Dudley Port Primitive Methodist Chapel was built in 1845 on the corner of Tividale Street, and was demolished in August 1905 to make way for its replacement, seen below. *(Sylvia Allcock collection)*

An architect's drawing of the 1905 chapel built on the corner of Tividale Street, Dudley Port, now replaced with the Methodist Centre, Dudley Port, which opened in 1991. The last service in this building was held on 3 November 1990. *(Sylvia Allcock collection)*

A Sunday School anniversary at Tividale Street in the early 1970s, beneath the lower part of the legend 'They that wait upon the Lord, shall renew their strength'. *(Sylvia Allcock collection)*

The choir at Tividale Street on 18 October 1980 when the Tividale Street Chapel reopened after some renovations. *(Sylvia Allcock collection)*

It is important not to confuse the Tividale Street (Primitive) Methodist chapel with its neighbour, the Dudley Port (Wesleyan) Methodists. In 1990 the two congregations combined and used this chapel while the new Methodist Centre, Dudley Port, was built on the Tividale Street site. On moving to the latter, these two buildings were demolished. *(Marje Taylor)*

A Sunday School anniversary at the Dudley Port (ex-Wesleyan) Chapel, beneath the 'Love Never Faileth' legend in the 1950s. *(Sylvia Allcock collection)*

The Revd John Barrett can be seen on the right in this picture of the stone-laying ceremony at Tividale Street, 28 April 1991. The new Methodist Centre was opened on 9 November that year. *(Sylvia Allcock collection)*

Sunday School anniversary at the Methodist Centre, Dudley Port, 27 June 2004. The minister, the Revd Pat Davies, and the organist, Marjorie Taylor, are on the left. The service was led by the speaker, Joy Forrest. Traditional white dresses, white shirts, blue ties and blue sashes prevail. *(NW)*

A short distance from the Tividale Street chapel was another Wesleyan chapel, in Hopkins Street. Sometimes known as the Burnt Tree Methodist Chapel, it became a remote outpost of the Dudley Circuit. The foundation stone was laid in 1876 but the chapel was not officially opened until 29 January 1877. (This picture was taken in 1976 to put on the cover of a centenary brochure.) The chapel has now closed but the building still stands. *(Ray Anstis collection)*

The congregation at Hopkins Street organised a Black Country pageant to mark their centenary on 3 April 1976. In the centre of the back row is Fred Pratt, the Sunday School Superintendent who organised the event. *(Ray Anstis collection)*

13 Woodside
Anniversaries & the Boys' Brigade

The many chapels of Dudley will have to be explored in a subsequent volume, but let us pause here in the Woodside/Holly Hall area of Dudley to enjoy a Sunday School anniversary and include a mention of the Boys' Brigade.

John Wesley first visited Dudley in 1749 and the first Wesleyan meeting house was built in Dudley's King Street in his lifetime, in 1788. Woodside was probably the second Wesleyan Methodist chapel to be built in the Dudley area, when a small building was erected in Hall Street in 1812. The building seen overleaf was built in 1890, after the Anglicans had arrived at St Augustine's (1884), and the Primitive Methodists had arrived at The Square in 1882. As usual it was mining subsidence that had caused problems for the original chapel. The replacement building, opened in July 1890, was designed by J.B. Marsh and built by Webb & Round, both Dudley firms. A Sunday School was added in 1929.

Woodside Methodists held their traditional Sunday School anniversary on 9 May 2004. The children and some members of the choir stand behind Gill Conway (choir mistress), the Revd Pat Nimmo and Lynda Bradbury (Sunday School Superintendent). *(NW)*

Church Secretary at Woodside in 2004 is Bill Jones, seen here next to the chapel's banner. *(NW)*

Woodside Methodist Chapel, Hallchurch Road, Dudley, as it is today – an 1890 building with 1929 extension. *(NW)*

The Boys' Brigade band leads a Sunday School anniversary procession around Woodside and Holly Hall, 1960s. The route invariably led past the Primitive Methodist chapel in The Square, a few hundred yards from the Wesleyan chapel. *(Roy Evans)*

Woodside's other chapel, the 'Chapel on the Square', built by the Primitive Methodists in 1882. The brickwork of this chapel was particularly attractive, with headers and stretchers in alternate blue and red, but it has now been rendered, and is used by a Pentecostal congregation. *(NW)*

This picture not only shows the brickwork of Woodside's 'Chapel on the Square', mentioned above, but also introduces the Boys' Brigade. Boys' Brigade and Girls' Brigade were more common at chapels than Scouts and Guides. This particular company was formed in 1952 as the 10th South Staffs Co., later becoming the 1st Dudley Co. Other Dudley companies were at Lodge Farm and Noah's Ark in Netherton and at Dudley Wood. The company eventually transferred to the Hallchurch Road chapel. *(Roy Evans)*

Girls' Brigade at Woodside Methodist Church was started in 1976. Captain Christine Conway and her daughters are in the picture, taken in the mid-1980s. One of Christine's daughters re-appears as the choir-mistress in the picture on page 87! *(Brian Conway's collection)*

The Boys' Brigade and Girls' Brigade had quite a high profile in Dudley after Brian Conway bought this ex-RAF Bedford bus and painted it in blue and red (Brigade colours). It was used for many years until seat belt legislation rendered it obsolete, and is seen here at the West Midlands BB & GB District Camping Centre at Duffryn. *(Brian Conway)*

14 Netherton
More Chapels than Pubs!

For some reason Netherton was never granted recognition in the form of an Urban District Council, yet it has been a sizeable community with a remarkable number of social institutions, including chapels. Their names possess a poetic quality: Messiah, Sweet Turf, Noah's Ark, the Swan Street Mission, for example, as well as the more common Ebenezer, Trinity and Providence. A Sunday School Union hymn of 1868 contains the lines:

> May Sweet Turf join with Cinder Bank, and Ebenezer swell the rank;
> And May St John's and Primrose Hill, With Noah's Ark their stations fill.

> And may Church Road and Darby Hand, All join in one harmonious band;
> Bow down Thine ear O God of Grace, And bless us in this market place.

The early presence of Dissenters is embedded in legend and the place name Baptist End. It is said that it was here that Cromwell's troops paused to pray before laying siege to Dudley Castle. Later the presence of miners and metal-workers encouraged the spread of Methodism and evangelical missions.

The Baptists have a long and complex history in Netherton, stretching back to 1654. The first Messiah Baptist chapel in Cinder Bank was built in 1746. This building, on the main road from Dudley to Netherton, was the product of Baptist reorganisation in the 1820s. It was built in 1831 and closed on 7 October 1979 when it became unsafe, but part of the site has been retained as a burial ground and memorial to the chapel.
(Dudley Archives)

The Particular Baptists at Sweet Turf Chapel in Netherton traced their history back to a congregation of thirteen established in 1810. They were celebrating their centenary when this picture was taken to appear in a 1910 Netherton Sunday School Exhibition programme. In recent years it has been used by the Champions' Church and the front has been altered.
(Albert Willetts)

In 1864 a General Baptist congregation in Netherton was formed by folks who broke away from the Strict Baptists at Sweet Turf. They built this chapel, the Ebenezer, in St Andrews Street, it opened in February 1865. A school room was added at the back in 1875. A few decades ago it was in decline, but with some help from the pastor at the Ebenezer, Coseley (see page 71), it has revived and has been refurbished. *(NW)*

At the end of the war prefabs were built at Lodge Farm in the Blackbrook Valley behind Netherton. By 1949 the construction of a permanent housing estate was underway. Some Baptists at Sweet Turf in Netherton, led by Mr A.J. Wilkinson, decided to create a Sunday School for the estate, using a builder's site hut. This was transformed into the little chapel or school hall seen here, which opened on 11 March 1950. *(NW)*

Members of the congregation worked hard to create a community church, and Ray and Madge Cole eventually found themselves running successful Boys' and Girls' Brigades. *Left:* The boys are seen left at camp in Guernsey. *Below:* The Boys' Brigade lead a parade around the Lodge Farm Estate in the 1950s. (Note prefab in background.) Half a century later the little chapel still struggles to serve the tight knit community of the estate.
(Madge & Ray Cole)

The Cole Street Methodists

Legend tells us that nailers from Derbyshire came to the Withymoor area and helped establish the scattered settlement known as Derby Hand or Darby End. They may have brought an interest in Methodism with them and possibly attended Wesleys meetings in Dudley.

A scythe-maker named John Griffin helped form the Darby End Building Society and bought land on which members could build a home when circumstances permitted. A Darby End Methodist Society existed by 1810. Ten years later the society bought land from John Griffin's widow and started to build a chapel. The Darby End Wesleyan Chapel was opened on 1 April 1821 and for the next forty years was both chapel and Sunday School.

The Sunday School building was opened in August 1861 and was also used as a day school until local board schools were built. Over the years many Darby End activities were centred at the chapel: for example, a cricket club, Death Club, Band of Hope, concerts and 'lantern services' (services with lantern picture slides). Another familiar part of the story concerned the threat of mining subsidence, although the chapel was never undermined. Nearby workings eventually pulled the ground and the chapel was affected. By the turn of the century rebuilding and extending became necessary.

The chapel reopened on 29 February 1904, redesigned by W.F. Edwards and rebuilt by Messrs Jakeman and Round. One young Sunday School student at the time was Bert Beard, who four years later chose to become a Sunday School teacher. He went on to become Superintendent, and on 30 March 1918 he and Annie Overton were the first couple to be married at the chapel – to which he devoted all his spare time. Years later he wrote a detailed history of the chapel; it is now a family heirloom awaiting publication.

With the Methodist reunification of 1933 the chapel had to drop the word Wesleyan and it became Cole Street Chapel to distinguish itself from its Primitive neighbour, Providence (now at the Black Country Living Museum). Five years later a

fund was started to replace the building once again. The war intervened and the final service in the old chapel did not take place until 14 May 1950.

Services moved to the school room until the new chapel was opened on 3 October 1959.

The front of the Cole Street Chapel, Netherton, as it was from 1921 until 1950. *(Bert Beard collection)*

The new chapel at Cole Street, Netherton, was opened on 3October 1959 – a forerunner of 1960s chapel design. The main hall has an altar at one end and stage facilities at the other. *(Bert Beard collection)*

The Sunday School anniversary of 20 June 2004 took the form of a presentation of *Joseph and the Amazing Technicolor Dreamcoat*, interrupted by congregational hymns and a sermon – making good use of the stage area. *(NW)*

Trinity, Church Street, Netherton

Twelve members of the Cole Street congregation seem to have decided in 1865 that there was need for another Wesleyan venture close to the centre of Netherton, despite the existence of another chapel in St Johns Street since 1848.

From temporary accommodation in a bakehouse they moved to a plot of land fronted by Church Street, and constructed a schoolroom/chapel on the back of this land – now a lawn. The building was much affected by mining subsidence and by the early 1890s meetings had to be held elsewhere. In 1893 a corrugated iron chapel was purchased second hand from Trinity Congregational Chapel in Birmingham. The bricks from the old Sunday School were used to build a new school, which formed the cellar-like foundations for the iron building; this was therefore able to stand level with Church Street. This housed the congregation until 1912 when it was sold – probably to provide the folks of Gornal with a cinema! (See page 26.)

Construction of the present brick building began in July 1912 and was completed for an opening in January 1913. The name Trinity has only been in use since 1991, when the Church Street congregation joined forces with the folks from St John's.

'Trinity' Wesleyan Chapel in Church Street, Netherton.
(*Cyril Wright collection*)

Although the interior of Trinity, Netherton, has not changed dramatically this picture is a reminder that painting out the scrolls of text on the walls of chapels does somehow change the atmosphere. *(Cyril Wright collection)*

Trinity Chapel, Netherton, preserves the tradition of flower festivals and musical events. Here we see the City of Wolverhampton Brass Band and conductor James Holmes presenting a concert in the chapel on 15 May 2004. *(NW)*

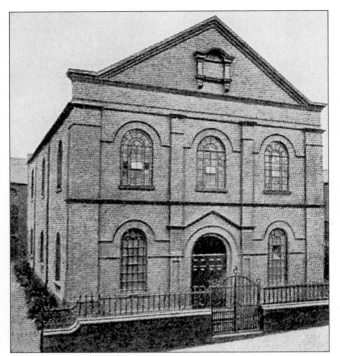

St John's Chapel in St John's Street, Netherton, was built in 1848, but the congregation first formed in 1827. It was originally a Methodist New Connexion Chapel. A Sunday School building was added and much rebuilding went on at the time of its fiftieth anniversary in 1898. The last service was held on 31 December 1990 and the congregation transferred to Trinity in Church Street. The chapel was then sold to an independent Pentecostal congregation who have carried out some restoration of the interior. *(Muriel Woodhouse collection)*

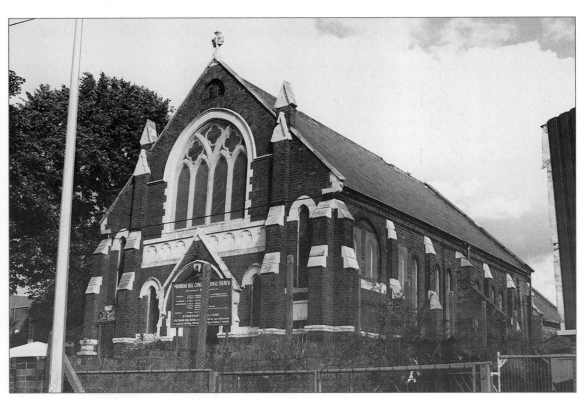

Primrose Hill. The Congregationalists in this part of Netherton first met in a cottage and were led by a J.F. Watkins. A chapel was built in 1871 but this was wrecked by the effects of mining (see page 13). This building was erected in 1887 and, despite being no longer level, is still being used today by an Independent Evangelical congregation. *(NW)*

Noah's Ark, Cradley Road, Netherton, traces its history back to a small group of Primitive Methodists who began meeting in 1843 – worshipping in each other's homes, referred to as arks. A chapel was built on this site in 1851, and a Sunday School in 1861. Both suffered the effects of subsidence as the result of mining. The school was rebuilt in 1896 and this building was completed in 1925. *(NW)*

The elegance of its interior could not save Noah's Ark, and it closed after the last service on 14 March 2004, conducted by the Revd Kate McCleland. At one time the congregation had supported a Band of Hope, a Women's Guild, a drama society, Bible study groups, youth clubs, Boys' Brigade and an Anti-Cigarette League. *(NW)*

The stone-laying ceremony at Noah's Ark on 16 March 1925, when construction of the chapel seen on the previous page began. Its predecessor, wrecked by subsidence, had been demolished and cleared by volunteers from the congregation. The building in the background is the Sunday School building of 1898. *(Chapel collection)*

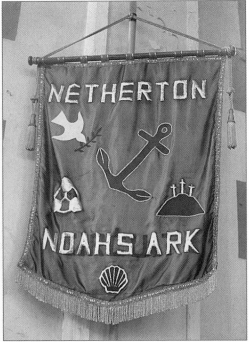

Left: John Dacre and Joan Bowen enjoyed the last wedding at Noah's Ark on 6 March 2004. *(NW)*
Above: Noah's Ark banner. *(NW)*

The People's Mission, Swan Street, Netherton, 2004. In the mid-1890s a group of Baptists from Messiah Chapel, Cinder Bank, formed a new independent congregation and rented a field in Swan Street. In just forty-two days in 1898 they erected one of Messrs Cooper's corrugated iron chapel kits. This building, replacing the tin chapel, was opened on 10 February 1934. It was built by W. Tilley for £3,800. *(NW)*

At the Children's Celebration of 13 June 2004 members of the Sunday School and congregation, led by Brian Payton, pose beneath the People's Mission banner, organ and the scroll legend: 'Enter His Courts With Praise'. The Swan Street Mission was famous for its Sunday School and its choirs. *(NW)*

F.G. Perkins took this picture of the first People's Mission Hall in Swan Street, Netherton for the 1910 Netherton Sunday Schools Exhibition programme. It was a classic tin tabernacle of 1898 vintage supplied by Messrs Cooper of London. (See the chapter on tin tabernacles for more information.) When the 1934 replacement was built the tin building continued to be used for Sunday School purposes, until it was demolished to make way for a new manse. *(Albert Willetts collection)*

A Pentecostal congregation, led by the Revd Desmond McDonald, which first met in Kate's Hill, Dudley, now uses the old St John's Chapel (see page 98). The picture was taken in July 2004. *(NW)*

15 Cradley Heath & Cradley

Cradley Heath and Cradley face one another across the river Stour – the southern boundary of the Black Country. Both communities supported a number of chapels, but at the time of writing Cradley Heath is about to lose its last Methodist church.

Perhaps life has never been easy. In a booklet published in 1906 the local Primitive Methodist circuit of seven chapels reflected on its progress: the two largest chapels, the Clocktower at Cradley Heath and the chapel in New Street, Quarry Bank, had both been destroyed by mining subsidence. The little chapel at Hayes Lane had been destroyed by a storm. Perhaps the folks in the New Connexion felt they were doing better as they planned a huge Sunday School building at Five Ways, but they would be shocked today to see that their chapel and the Sunday School building have both been abandoned eyesores for years. It has been rumoured that a new ring road will remove them, but the more immediate effect of this planned road is the closure of the distinctive Salvation Army citadel – said to be the second-oldest surviving citadel in the country.

To the south of the Stour, in Cradley, several chapels have completely disappeared but on the other hand we can celebrate the survival of two ragged schools!

The Clocktower Chapel, in Graingers Lane. Primitive Methodism arrived in Cradley Heath in the 1820s and this chapel was built in 1841. A gallery was added in 1854 and the clock-tower was built in 1860. By 1888 the building had begun to subside and the tower was no longer perpendicular. The tower had to be demolished and the congregation transferred to an 1873 Sunday School building on the opposite side of the road. (*Muriel Woodhouse collection*)

For a time the Primitive Methodists of Graingers Lane, Cradley Heath, met in the Sunday School building of 1873, located on the site of the car park seen in this 2004 photograph. The foundation stones of the chapel seen here were laid on 2 October 1905. Construction began of an ambitious complex consisting of chapel, vestries, church hall, Young Men's Institute and Temperance Hall, in the fashionable Tudor Gothic style, adding up to a £4,500 bill. The architect was Messrs Ewen Harper & Brother, and the builder was Joseph Meredith of Cradley Heath.

It was opened on 24 September 1906. A 60ft square tower made the building even more church-like. The clock had to be added later as funds ran out at the time of building the chapel. The interior was spacious and elegant, with a raked wooden floor, oak panelling, stained glass windows and impressive organ. *(NW)*

The Revd John T. Wilkinson and his superintendents, Messrs Head and Fletcher, and Sunday School staff at Graingers Lane, 1927. *(Muriel Woodhouse collection)*

The Graingers Lane chapel was supported by three branches of the Woodhouse family, each associated with a local chainmaking firm. (They had a pact that while in chapel they would never discuss business!) There are at least three Woodhouse ladies here among the members of the 1927 Ladies Class. *(Muriel Woodhouse collection)*

The Graingers Lane congregation on 6 June 2004, posing in front of the Norman & Beard organ, which was dedicated by Ernest Stevens on 3 February 1910, one of several local chapel organs partly paid for by Andrew Carnegie. Graingers Lane Methodist Church closed in 2004, with a final service on 18 July. *(NW)*

The New Connexion came to Cradley Heath in 1836 with the opening of Bethel Chapel in Scolding Green. In 1885 the Society built this large chapel, known as Christ Church, at Four Ways – mainly through the generosity of Joseph Witley, whose name is commemorated in the Sunday School hall seen below, built in 1910. The last service at Christ Church was held on 30 August 1970, and both buildings now await demolition.
(NW & Bob Broadfield)

The Baptist chapel in Corngreaves Road, Cradley Heath, near the Four Ways, is a striking building in the red brick and terracotta stonework tradition, seen here in 2004. It has an interesting history. The congregation was established by Jabez Tunnicliffe when he left the Cradley Baptists in 1833. They built a chapel – the first in Cradley Heath – in 1834. This building dates from 1904. The chapel was also the first in the Black Country to have a black pastor, George Cosens; he replaced Tunnicliffe in 1837. *(NW)*

The Four Ways Baptists' Junior and Senior Christian Endeavour put on a concert in the early 1930s. The devil, top right, was Philip Bytheway who became church secretary, and the King of Hearts was Doug Hingley who met his future wife at the chapel – Phyllis Atwell, seated second from left. *(Doug Hingley)*

In the mid-1960s the Four Ways Baptists won the Midlands Scripture Exam for the first and only time: it was often won by Sweet Turf from Netherton. The shield is proudly displayed by four members of the Marsh family, Philip Bytheway (church secretary, top left), John Broadhurst, Hilary Smart, Ann George, the Minister, the Revd Derek Taylor, and others. *(Doug Hingley collection)*

The Young Ladies' class from Four Ways Baptist Chapel, Cradley Heath, in the late 1920s – in the days when chapels had classes and activities running every moment of the week. *(Doug Hingley collection)*

Some Black Country chapels achieved great architectural dignity through the absolute simplicity and classicism of their design. Others, like the Baptist chapel at Cradley, were the opposite and obviously competed to be a cathedral among chapels. It was designed by local architect A.T. Butler and was opened in February 1901. To say that Cradley has a complicated nonconformist history is an understatement, but the Baptists generally traced their independent history back to 1798, although it was 1803 before they had their first chapel built in the High Street. The congregation and the Baptist ministers of Cradley often fell out, and the erection of this building marked a more settled period that began in the twentieth century. It closed in the 1960s. *(Peter Barnsley)*

Dissenters in the south west of the Black Country who had previously met at Cradley Forge, at what was known as the Pensnett Meeting House, purchased land at Netherend in 1794 to build a new chapel. It was opened on 15 May 1796. It became known as the Park Lane chapel and eventually declared itself to be Unitarian. The chapel went through a major rebuild in 1864, in which extra bays were added and the tower moved from one end of the building to the other. This picture was taken in 2004. *(NW)*

The Park Lane chapel at Netherend has remained resolutely independent and Unitarian although it now meets on a monthly basis. The congregation is seen here on 9 May 2004 at the anniversary service when the preacher was Margaret Phelan. *(NW)*

The Wesleyan chapel in Cradley (Trinity) has vanished, and so has the Primitive Methodist chapel (Bethesda). However, the New Connexion chapel, Providence, has survived with a vengeance and a new chapel was built at Windmill Hill, which opened on 29 June 1963. The other interesting survivor is the People's Mission at Overend, which began life in 1905 and moved to Banner Street in 1911. The Mission merged with the congregation from Bethesda in 1971 and entered the Methodist fold. Trinity merged with Overend in 1995. This 2004 picture shows the effect of a new lobby, added in 1977, on the Banner Street premises. *(NW)*

Sunday School children led by Deb Westwood at the Overend Methodist Mission's Anniversary Service, 16 May 2004. *(NW)*

Left: The little chapel in Belle Vale was in Halesowen rather than Cradley, but both Belle Vale and Hayseech served remote parts of the Stour Vale and have now vanished. Belle Vale opened in 1886 and closed in 1994. *(Jill Guest)*

Below: Hayseech Chapel in a narrow section of the Stour Vale. *(Jill Guest)*

Bottom: The Hayseech chapel choir of the 1940s, with Tom Harris on the organ and Bob While, the Sunday School Superintendent. Virtually everyone in the picture is related. *(Jill Guest)*

Ragged Schools

In 1812 the Ragged School Movement was started by John Pounds (1766–1839) in Portsmouth with two aims: to provide a simple place of worship for the poorest people, and to teach those same people to read so that they could read the Bible. Ragged was an adjective often used at the time to describe an underclass locked into a life of squalor and poverty.

The idea spread in the nineteenth century, after being popularised by the Revd Thomas Guthrie, who synthesised John Pound's ideas with some similar ideas developed in Scotland. The Ragged School Union was established in 1844, led by Lord Shaftesbury. Between then and the passing of the 1870 Education Act about 350 Ragged Schools were opened. The schools preached evangelical Christianity, taught literacy and numeracy and a number of life-skills – all provided free for those too poor to acquire any other education. When the 1870 School Boards began their work the Ragged Schools became much more like conventional Sunday Schools.

A large Ragged School opened in Wolverhampton in 1852 and there were others in Bilston, Sedgley and Brierley Hill, for example, but the only two survivors in the Black Country exist quite close to one another in Cradley at High Town and Two Gates.

Marion and John Dunn of the High Town Ragged School, Cradley, with the Scripture Class of 1980. (*Marion Dunn collection*)

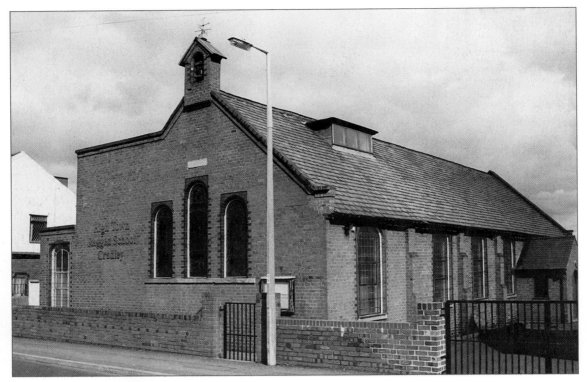

High Town Ragged School, Mapletree Lane, Cradley as it is today, in 2004. *(NW)*

High Town Ragged School, Cradley. The cast of *Pearl, the Fisher Maid* is at the back of the old classroom – where the chapel's kitchen is now. The picture was taken in about 1917. *(Marion Dunn collection)*

A Cradley High Town Ragged School anniversary, *c.* 1950. In the centre of the picture stands Caleb Southall. On the right is Bert Head, local JP and Secretary of the Chainmakers' union. Top right is Walter Hodgetts, children's choirmaster. *(Marion Dunn collection)*

Like many chapels who no longer have a Sunday School, the High Town Ragged School has started holding Anniversary re-unions. Marion (chapel secretary) and John Dunn (chapel Superintendent) and the choir, with pianist Gill Richards and organist Jonathan Salter, celebrate the re-union on 2 May 2004. *(John James)*

The Two Gates Ragged School, Cradley, was created in 1867 although its origins seem lost in legend. Local benefactors Messrs Hingley and Homfray may have fallen out with the congregation, as it seemed at one point that the building might be handed over to another denomination. The congregation maintained it independence as a ragged school. *(NW)*

The Two Gates Ragged School still maintains a very independent existence, owing its survival to the tenacity of Clifford Willets (Superintendent 1932–81) and his daughter, Hazel (1981–92). A reunion choir was mustered to celebrate the anniversary on 21 June 2004. *(NW)*

16   Brierley Hill
Chapels on a Tea-Towel

On 30 January 1971 over 800 people packed into the new Methodist church in Brierley Hill to celebrate its opening. The £50,000 modern multi-purpose building, designed by John P. Osborne & Sons, and built by Bruce Tipper Ltd, was to be known as Brierley Hill Methodist Church, but old traditions die hard and many people still describe it as Bank Street. This is unfortunate, because Bank Street was only one of the six congregations that united to create this new congregation.

This tale of closures and amalgamations is celebrated in a tea-towel (pronounced tay cloth in the Black Country) and a journey into the world of Brierley Hill's chapels can begin by exploring the tea-towel. There was no shortage of chapels in Brierley Hill – providing for all brands of Methodism, and running the full range of nonconformity from the long established Baptists to the independent evangelicals in their missions. Some were on each other's doorstep in 'central' Brierley Hill, but others prospered because Brierley Hill was not really a single entity. It included of a number of outlying communities all experiencing a varying degree of feeling separate from Brierley Hill.

Six ladies from the Brierley Hill Methodist Craft Group pose in June 2004 with the tea towel produced to commemorate the chapels brought together in the new church in Bank Street. Left to right: Beryl Totney from Moor Street, Jean Harris from Bank Street, Lillian Davis from Albion Street Congregationalists, Doreen Gripton from Brockmoor, Gladys George from Hill Street and Brenda Hemming from Silver End. They are standing in front of the window brought from the former chapel in Bank Street now incorporated into the new building. *(NW)*

The Bank Street Methodist Chapel, Brierley Hill

In about 1811 or 1812 a Wesleyan Society was established in the Brierley Hill area – meeting in the home of Samuel Cooper in what we now know as Level Street, although Societies existed in all the villages surrounding Brierley Hill by that date. A preaching room was provided by Noah Pearson in 1823 in a building that was located on the site now occupied by Walter Smith's shop near Five Ways. This was temporary accommodation used while the congregation grew and prepared to build a more permanent home.

The Wesleyan's new home was in Bank Street – the new chapel opening on 11 October 1829. The Prims had already opened their chapel at Round Oak in 1821, but the Wesleyans were confident enough to build a chapel with a seating capacity of 668, and a Sunday School building. Like most societies, the folks at Bank Street put schemes in hand with great confidence and faith and then afterwards battled with the debts they incurred. Their faith was also put to the test by the effects of subsidence. Eventually the trustees resorted to purchasing mineral rights, as well as struggling with repairs, to save the chapel.

Bank Street suffered occasional closures and re-openings – the last of which was on 8 January 1950, following a complete restoration. Final demolition came in 1969.

The Wesleyan Chapel in Bank Street, Brierley Hill.
(*Stan Hill collection*)

Closures & Amalgamations

The chapels at Brockmoor, Hill Street and Moor Street agreed to amalgamate with Bank Street on 5 September 1965. They were joined in 1970 by the congregation from Silver Street while the new united church in Bank Street was being built. While the new building was under construction, the Methodists joined the Congregationalists in Albion Street in joint worship, and when the Congregationalists 'closed' in Albion Street many of them came along to Bank Street.

Of the six chapels appearing on the tea-towel, the one in Bent Street was the first to close. The last service was held on 2 February 1945. (The premises were later used by the St John Ambulance Brigade.) The Primitive Methodists at Bent Street traced their history back to early days in the 1820s at Round Oak.

The Prims at Round Oak had a part in establishing the congregation that met at the other end of Brierley Hill in what became Hill Street. Work on the chapel began in 1853, and it was opened on 5 November 1854. Just 110 years later the chapel faced demolition with the advance of the multi-storey flats and the congregation faced merger with Bank Street. As Brierley Hill gives way to Brettell Lane one passes through the hamlet of Silver End. The Primitive Methodists in this area were sufficiently organised by the mid-1850s to obtain land and build a chapel and Sunday School. It was opened on 29 June 1856, although it did not adopt the name Silver Street until 1891. Moor Street and Brockmoor will be described separately.

Silver Street Chapel in Silver End held its last service on 19 July 1970. Five years later it was being used by the Mormon Church, as seen in this photograph. The early 1980s brought the threat of demolition and the Mormons found a new home in Quarry Bank. Although the site was scheduled for industrial use new houses have now been built on the site. (*Stan Hill collection*)

Moor Lane Primitive Methodist Chapel

Today Beryl Totney is an Assistant Steward ('that means I wash the pots') at the Brierley Hill Methodist Church. Time and time again chapel attendance seems related to family history and tradition, so Beryl can soon take the listener back to days before the closures when she attended the Moor Lane Primitive Methodist Chapel. Her father and mother had first met at the church as children in the Sunday School, and Mum came from the Prince family. At one time the church was filled with Princes and other families such as the Myles. Dad, Percy Walters, was later a trustee. Percy had married Sara Prince at the chapel, just as Beryl later married her husband, Jack Totney, at the chapel. Beryl still possesses a Sunday School Anniversary Programme of 10 May 1964 when she is listed as presiding over the event, and Jack is identified as 'choirmaster' ('He had a way of making the children sing,' explains Beryl.)

A Primitive Methodist congregation in the Moor Lane area began to assemble in the 1830s and the first chapel appears to have been built in 1839, at the junction of Moor Lane and Norwood Road. Moor Lane later became Moor Street and the chapel changed in line with this in 1891. It also went through numerous rebuilding programmes, followed by reopenings in 1865, 1878 and 1898. Major repairs and renovations were still taking place as late as the mid-1950s. All this demanded endless fund-raising. Ten years later, in 1965, the trustees were agreeing to the amalgamation proposals and the closure of their church.

After closure the site was acquired by the Council and the chapel was demolished.

The frontage of Moor Lane chapel was quite grand and must have been the result of one of its numerous rebuilds in the second half of the nineteenth century. (*Beryl Totney collection*)

Staff and pupils of Moor Lane Sunday School, *c.* 1907. The lad on the right of the front row is Percy Walters who later became a trustee of the chapel. His future wife, Sara Prince, peeps out round the brim of that hat a few feet to his right. *(Beryl Totney collection)*

Wesleyan Sunday School parade in Brockmoor. For many years Harold Jeavons was a trustee and hard-working Sunday School Superintendent, and he is seen here on the right. *(Keith Jeavons collection)*

The Sand Hole: Brockmoor Methodist Chapel

Wesleyan Methodism seems to have taken root in Brockmoor as early as the mid-1790s, when the village was just embarking on its industrial transformation. Right from the beginning its fortunes were linked to the involvement of key local families and this remained so throughout the congregation's history. Early reports describe the congregation as being segregated by gender when meeting for worship, although there is some confusion about where they first met.

Legend has it that their first meeting place was built on sand, or rather that the sand was removed and sold and the chapel occupied the sand hole. The building belonged to one of the founders of the church, William Beckley, and was first used by the Kilhamites, or New Connexion Methodists. In 1838 he sold it to trustees of the Wesleyan persuasion. When the Kingswinford Branch of the Oxford, Worcester & Wolverhampton Railway was built twenty years later on adjoining land, the Brierley Hill to Wordsley road was raised to cross the railway, and the church and its Sunday School seemed even more 'down a hole'.

The Sunday School building was rebuilt in 1886–7 and increased its capacity from 100 to 300 children. The actual cost was £475, as opposed to the £350 estimated, because of extra work required to establish foundations in the sand hole. The Brockmoor congregation was not wealthy and occasional leaps forward seem to have come about when a rising generation felt annoyed by their elders' complacency and made decisions to improve facilities. Thus it was that one Christmas morning young males in the choir decided it was time to rebuild the church, and they immediately set about fund-raising.

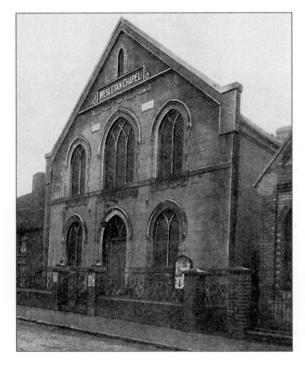

The rebuilt Wesleyan chapel of 1898 at Brockmoor, photographed in 1928 – no longer in its sand hole but level with the road. The adjacent Sunday School hall can just be seen on the right.
(Stan Hill collection)

The interior of the Wesleyan chapel at Brockmoor. The right-hand side of the chapel went through some modification but it remained more or less like this until its closure. After closure the organ was removed piece by piece and was taken to Pensnett Secondary School in Tiled House Lane.
(Kevin Gripton collection)

The new chapel was built in 1898 – lifting itself out of the sand hole and in fact standing well above the level of the road. Over £1,000 was spent, and although the building itself was substantial, much of the money must have been spent on the foundations. In 1900 a further £300 was spent on installing an organ. Little wonder that the trustees were much concerned with debt and fund-raising, although everything was paid for by 1928.

Brockmoor families that participated in all this included the Pearsons, the Clulows, the Clares, the Thompsons, the Gallimores, the Beckleys and the Jeavons. Many of these families became inter-related by marriage, and a meeting of the trustees must have seemed like a family conference. They were tradesmen and shopkeepers of Brockmoor and Brierley Hill, but without the wealth of the families that established the bigger businesses in the area. Brockmoor gazed upon the prosperity of Brierley Hill with some envy. What the folks in the sand hole thought of the Anglicans who built St John's Church on the opposite side of the road in 1845 is less clear.

In 1938 the sand hole congregation celebrated a centenary – looking back to 1838 when they had first taken possession of their building. The event was marked by opening a brand new Guild Hall at the back of the church. The £800 building was designed by local architect Stanley Griffiths and was built by Thomas Round of Amblecote. Improvements were also made to the church. Once again the trustees devoted hours to debt management and fund-raising! Up until the Second World War all this was rewarded with a thriving Sunday School and youth activities, well-patronised services, and an active Women's Guild meeting in its new Guild Hall.

Family history and loyal devotion to the chapel protected its independence but could not tackle the decline that seemed to set in by the 1950s. The chapel officially closed in 1965 when its dwindling congregation reluctantly merged with others in Brierley Hill, joining forces to build a new Methodist Centre. It was demolished, and nowadays new housing occupies the site.

A Survivor in Campbell Street

So many little chapels have disappeared or been converted to other use in the Black Country that it is a welcome surprise to drive down a back street and find a curious survivor. One such is the tiny chapel in Campbell Street, Brockmoor.

It declares its history on the front of the building: 'Erected 1861, restored 1905', but no times of service are to be found on its noticeboard. It also tells everyone that it is part of the Independent Wesleyan Reform Union, hoping perhaps that we are familiar with Methodist history and schisms within the movement. However, none of this should put off the investigator, for here in the twenty-first century is a preserved piece of chapel life that belongs to an earlier age.

The reformers seceded from the Wesleyan Methodist Church in 1849 – just twelve years before this chapel was built. One aspect of reform concerned independence and the power of the laity. Perhaps it is this that has guaranteed the survival of Campbell Street's chapel. Even today it seems to exist as the result of the enthusiasm of one man of independent character.

For the last twenty-two years Ernie Round has looked after his church and its congregation as if it was his family. He follows in the footsteps of David Woodhall, who died on 14 January 1987 having been Sunday School Superintendent and 'Church Leader' for forty-two years. In turn, David had taken over from his father, Henry James Woodhall.

Everything in the chapel is given in memory of someone who once supported it: the Bible commemorates Doris May Payne who died in 1995 aged 72, the hymn books are in memory of Dorothy Morgan who died in 1999. She and her husband 'worshipped at

Left: The modest exterior of Brockmoor's Campbell Street Wesleyan Reformed Chapel in 2004. *(NW)*

Opposite, top: Ernie Round at the Campbell Street chapel, 3 April 2004. The scroll on the rear wall of the chapel reads 'O Worship the Lord in the Beauty of Holiness'. Although tiny, the chapel has all the traditional features including a gallery, tiered choir stalls and elevated pulpit. *(NW)*

Opposite, bottom: The congregation seen at Campbell Street the following day: 4 April 2004. Left to right: Ernie Round, Harry Hale, Phyllis Hale at the organ, two visitors from Brazil, Edward Newton (the visiting preacher), Geoff Slater, David Broome and Joan Westwood. *(NW)*

the church for many years', the inscriptions tell us. The organ commemorates David Woodhall, and was purchased by Ernie Round in the belief that 'The Lord would provide', indeed, a few days after its purchase a bequest paid for it.

Not far away the Sand Hole Chapel drew large numbers, but Campbell Street appealed to those who cherished independence. It ended up with a very scattered congregation and was forced to have two church parades – one local and one far flung – organised to pass the homes of distant members. A man who once marched in the Boys' Brigade Band on such occasions recalls that he hated the second Campbell Street parade as it often lasted four hours!

Today this congregation has diminished and Ernie reckons that there may be under a dozen members, with often only half a dozen at the 6 o'clock Sunday service. The gallery is out of use, and the walls are much ravaged by damp, but preachers still come to Campbell – Street confirming Ernie's belief that the place 'still has some spirit'.

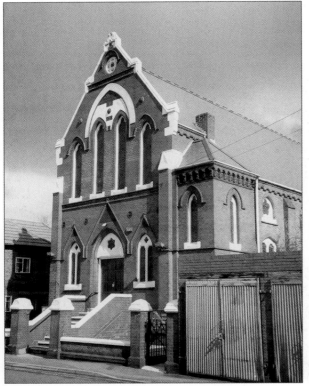

Above: The opening of the new Baptist chapel in Brierley Hill's South Street, 27 June 1964. Dr Payne, Secretary of the Baptist Union, is about to unveil a plaque commemorating Brierley Hill's oldest chapel. The Baptists are able to demonstrate history back to 1796. (The old chapel on this site, which had closed in 1947, was built in 1854.) The £10,000 building, in typical 1960s style, was designed by Roger Hodges who was a Baptist. *(NW collection)*

Left: The Congregational chapel was opened on 6 December 1882, although the Congregationalists go back much further. A year after becoming United Reform in 1973, their Sunday School was sold to the Jehovah's Witnesses. In 1976 the chapel itself was sold to the Assembly of God Pentecostals. *(NW)*

Fenton Street Gospel Hall & the William Street Free Church

In 1887 it seems that one Enoch Harris, an evangelist, took charge of the Gospel Union Tabernacle in Fenton Street, Brierley Hill. It was a wooden shed with an earth floor and very basic facilities. Enoch's evangelical zeal was matched by his determination to build something better. Today a plaque survives in the William Street building recalling that the large 600-seater Fenton Street building was built by Enoch Harris 'with his own hands'.

Enoch's brick building was known as the Gospel Hall, and it opened on 7 June 1896; it was officially registered as a place of worship three years later. Enoch's heroic efforts were recorded in a booklet called 'God and One Man' published by the *Christian Herald* in 1896. Much later the hall separated itself from the Gospel Union and became known as the Fenton Street Mission, describing its congregation as 'Christians – not otherwise designated'.

Like many chapels and missions, the Fenton Street hall's survival is linked with family history, and leadership was passed down to each succeeding generation. For example, leadership passed from Enoch to his son Isaac Harris. Today the congregation is led by Evelyn Price, who can recall the time of Isaac Harris, who must have died in the early 1930s. Evelyn's father, William Baker, was made Sunday School Superintendent in the 1920s at the age of 23, about ten years after coming to Fenton Street. Evelyn is reluctant to call herself leader but realises it is something she has inherited.

Fenton Street once had the largest Sunday School in the area and the 600-seater hall was packed, particularly when visited by well-known evangelists like 'Woodbine

Evelyn Price, left, and congregation at the William Street chapel, 23 May 2004. The plaques commemorate the opening at William Street in 1977 and the single-handed efforts of Enoch Harris in building the chapel's predecessor in Fenton Street in the 1880s. *(NW)*

Willie'. All this quickly changed in the 1960s when the area was redeveloped. The council did not originally seem interested in acquiring the hall or its land, and therefore the trustees were encouraged to refurbish and upgrade it so that the chapel became much more church-like. Wooden pews and pulpit were provided as well as a new ceiling and modern electric light.

It reopened on 26 January 1966, but in a cruel twist of fate the council then decided it did require the hall to be demolished, despite the obvious protests. A deal was stuck in which the congregation was given the chance to erect a new building in William Street. Sir Michael Higgs, the mission's solicitor, was confident that the council would pay sufficient for the replacement church to be built without creating any debt – something that nineteenth-century church builders would have regarded as a miracle. He joked that he expected to be made the church's first bishop.

The new building in William Street was designed by Michael John, who had family connections with the congregation. It was opened by William Baker on 18 June 1977, then proclaiming itself to be a Free Christian Church. Some items from Fenton Street were moved to William Street, along with the plaque recording the efforts of Enoch Harris.

Ironically a new church building did not generate a new congregation – the old congregation had melted away in all the changes that had taken place. Evelyn has felt that they have become custodians of the building and its history, while waiting to discover its way forward – including new uses to which the building might be put in the regeneration of Brierley Hill.

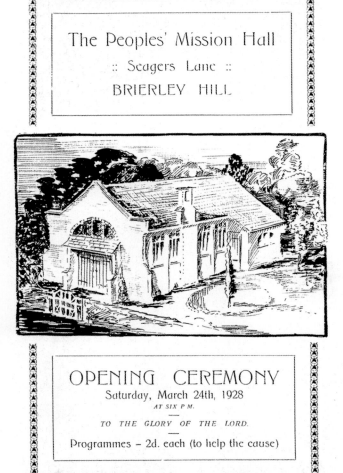

The Peoples' Mission Hall

:: Seagers Lane ::

BRIERLEY HILL

OPENING CEREMONY

Saturday, March 24th, 1928

AT SIX P M.

TO THE GLORY OF THE LORD.

Programmes – 2d. each (to help the cause)

The Seagars Lane Mission Hall was opened on 24 March 1928, as can be seen from this brochure. It was also known as the Glad Tidings Hall. From 1937 until 1946 it was also used by the Brierley Hill corps of the Salvation Army. Little seems to be known about the Seagars Lane Mission. In the 1950s its evangelical congregation was led by Pastor Cove, but no record has been found of its closure and subsequent demolition. Another Seagars Lane picture appears on page 11.

Heading west from Brierley Hill and Brockmoor we come to the villages of Bromley and Pensnett. The Wesleyan Methodist chapel was built in Bromley in 1828 when the area was becoming very industrialised. Like many chapels it was affected by mining and as early as 1941 it was decided to replace the building. At the end of 1959 the building collapsed – by which time construction of its replacement, on the other side of the road, had begun. *(Stan Hill collection)*

Anglicans and Methodists now share a church opposite the old Bromley Chapel. The new chapel/church (left) was built by Batham & Beddall and was designed by Stanley Griffiths. It was opened on 16 July 1960. To the right is the Sunday School building, erected in 1910. *(NW)*

A Primitive Methodist chapel opened at Shut End in 1832, in an area that was extensively mined and dominated by the Oak Farm Ironworks. By the 1890s the chapel was in a very bad way and its leaders had also fallen out with the ministers of the local circuit. The result was that the Pensnett men built this new chapel on Common Side near the High Oak calling it an Independent Methodist Church. It opened on 29 July 1894. A Conacher organ was added in 1909 with a Carnegie grant. In 2004 the chapel is used by a Church of God of Prophecy congregation. *(NW)*

The Conacher organ at Pensnett photographed in 1997 just before its removal for preservation, the Independents having ceased to use the chapel in 1994. In 1909 it had cost £300. *(John Lloyd)*

In Kingswinford the Wesleyan Methodists built this chapel in Moss Grove in 1853, and the Primitive Methodists built their chapel in Mount Pleasant five years later. Both chapels later had Sunday School buildings added. The Moss Grove chapel received this new façade in 1903.

By the 1960s it was obvious to many that the congregations should amalgamate. Mount Pleasant closed on 11 July 1965 and members transferred to Moss Grove, until that building closed on 12 June 1966.

The following Saturday, 18 June 1966, the Kingswinford Methodist Society dedicated its new premises in Stream Road, seen below. The latter soon hit the headlines by providing an all night café on Fridays for passing motorists heading for holidays in the South West!
(Stan Hill collection)

The first Primitive Methodist chapel was built at the end of Chapel Street, Wordsley, in 1833 and this one in New Street, its successor, was opened on 18 February 1883 – fifty years later. The first sermon was delivered by the Revd Charles Dudley, of Wolverhampton. (He had grown up as a member of the former chapel.) Charles Dudley's son, the Rev John Dudley, was able to preach the sermon at the chapel's centenary in 1983! The Sunday School at the rear of the chapel was considerably rebuilt in 1954 by J.M. Tate & Sons – well-known Methodists from Colley Gate. Modifications to the nineteenth-century interior of the chapel were carried out in the 1960s. When this picture was taken in 2004 it seemed that the chapel was threatened with closure. *(NW)*

The first Methodist chapel built in Amblecote was erected in 1831 in Brettell Lane. It was eventually inhabited by New Connexion Methodists and is now the site of a Christian Centre. The displaced Wesleyans eventually opened a chapel in High Street in 1840, greatly extending it in the 1870s. This new frontage was provided in 1993 when the premises were modernised. *(NW)*

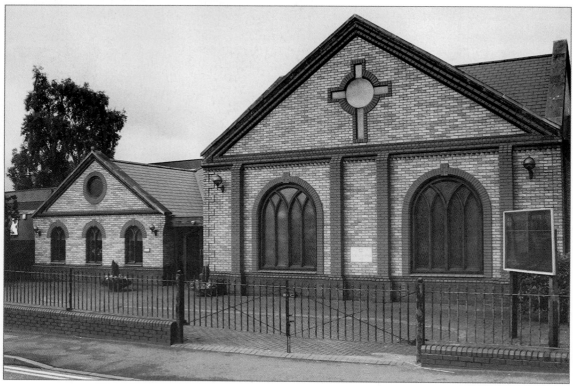

17   Contrasts in The Lye

Like its neighbour, Cradley, the old urban district of Lye and Wollescote took the Black Country into northern Worcestershire. As such it enjoyed a reputation or notoriety that fostered the illusion that the township was on the very edge of civilisation, and that the natives lived in 'mud houses'. The inhabitants of Lye Waste were regarded as a particularly lawless and godless lot. It was fertile ground, therefore, for the Anglican Church, nonconformists, independents and the Salvation Army to come to save folks' souls.

Lye and Wollescote, absorbed into Stourbridge and then into Dudley, changed enormously in the 1960s. Many chapels closed and congregations were amalgamated. Here we have space to look at the results of these amalgamations, take in a closed chapel now turned to new use and to look at the lively survival of independent chapel life at the Bethel in Hill Street.

General Booth spent six weeks in The Lye and the Salvation Army was established in the area from 1881 onwards. A citadel was built in Church Street, but has been replaced with a modern building next door to the United Church.

The United Church in The Lye is a classic example of the success of mergers and amalgamations in the face of changing circumstances. Photographed here in 1995, it was opened in March 1979 as a result of mergers between Methodist chapels and the Zion United Reformed Church. Thus it is part of both the Stour Vale Circuit of Methodist Chapels and the Worcester & Hereford District of UR Churches! The building itself is interesting because it was converted to a place of worship after a previous incarnation as the local Liberal Club. Worshippers travel to the first floor in a lift and worship in a centrally heated double-glazed multi-purpose hall. For good historical measure it stands next door to the Salvation Army citadel. (NW)

When photographed in 2004 the Salem Chapel on Pedmore Road, The Lye, had re-opened as a furniture store, retaining many features of the chapel. Originally a Wesleyan Reform Union chapel, built in 1893, the chapel frontage was constructed of refractory bricks supplied by George King Harrison. Three generations of the Dickens family played the organ at Salem over a period of ninety years. It was designed by Owen Freeman, who also designed the Bethel Chapel, Hill Street, seen below in 2004. *(NW)*

Not exactly a tin tabernacle, but the Bethel Chapel did have a splendid corrugated iron Sunday School/hall built at the rear of the chapel. For many years painted bright blue, it was demolished just after this photograph was taken in July 2001. A magnificent community facility, built by Arthur Griffin of Wolverhampton, has been erected on the site, and was opened at Easter 2002. *(Bethel archives)*

The Bethel congregation has also preserved the chapel's banner (see page 20), and it is seen here in about 1990 forming the backdrop to Sunday School children taking part in the anniversary. *(Bethel archives)*

The Bethel choir with their choir master, Fred Durbin, in the late 1920s. The Bethel Chapel was a product of independent spirit and the tendency to break away from existing congregations. The founders, including Albert Perks, Martha Westwood and the Dickens family, first met in the latter's home. The present chapel, in Hill Street, was opened on 2 April 1900, and it is still a very vibrant place of worship over a century later. *(E. Shore via Bethel archives)*

Bandmaster Sam Dawes and the Lye Salvation Army Band pose in the old hall in Church Street, Lye, 1938. *(Bram Dunn collection)*

18   Blackheath, Old Hill & Halesowen

Amalgamations, closures and demolitions have much changed the chapel scene in the towns in the south of the Black Country. However, there is much to investigate – ranging from the new Methodist Centre in Blackheath, to fine classical chapels maintained by the Baptists in Bell End, and Beeches, Road Blackheath, together with an attractive Salvation Army Citadel, some unusual mission halls and some ex-chapels now enjoying new use, not forgetting the opposite: some buildings now converted to places of worship!

The Strict & Particular Baptists established themselves on the Rowley Regis side of Blackheath in 1828, led by Daniel Matthews (see page 47). They built this fine chapel, Providence, at Bell End, in 1876. The Alphagraphix van on the left reminds us that this manufacturer of card kits produces a kit to make a model of this chapel! *(Roger Crombleholme)*

On the other side of Blackheath, in Beeches Road, the Baptists formed a congregation in 1840. In June 1897 they began building the impressive Cave Adullam chapel, seen here in 2004. It has a striking interior with the gallery supported by cast-iron columns. *(NW)*

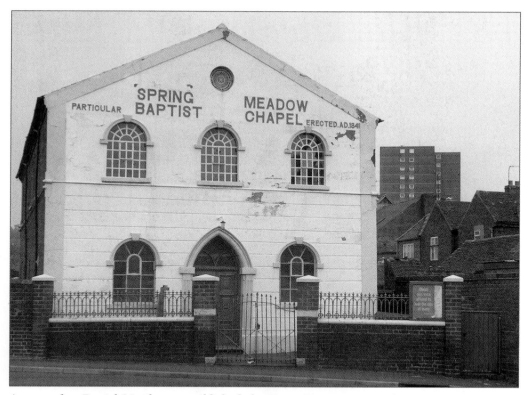

A year after Daniel Matthews established the Strict Baptists in Rowley Regis a group was formed in Old Hill. This also grew and prospered, building its first chapel in Spring Meadow in 1841, and enlarged to look like this is 1864. Since the mid-1980s, when this picture was taken, the front elevation has been rebuilt and the lettering has disappeared.
Below: The shell of Old Hill's Wesleyan chapel of 1904 vintage seen in 2004. *(NW)*

The organ at the front of the Old Hill Wesleyan Methodist Chapel looks suitably imposing in this photograph taken shortly before closure and removal of all fittings. During the 1980s BBC organist Nigel Ogden gave concerts on this organ. *(John Lloyd)*

Looking towards the altar in the Birmingham Road Methodist Chapel (New Connexion) in Blackheath. There is a strong external architectural similarity between this church and the Old Hill Wesleyan chapel and many others built in the 1890s/1900s. *(John Lloyd)*

On 6 July 1950 Reginald Dixon, of Blackpool fame, came to play the refurbished organ at Cocksheds Methodist Chapel, Malt Mill Lane, Blackheath. The congregation of this chapel has now merged with others to form the new Blackheath Central Church. *(Norman Hurley via Anthony Page)*

Halesowen has several ex-chapels that are now enjoying new use. The old Zion chapel is now an office building. The original Zion was opened in 1842 by New Connexion Methodists and closed in 1979. A Zion Pentecostal congregation began using it in 1981 but then moved to a new Christian Centre created in the former Webb-Ivory headquarters. *(NW)*

19   The Salvation Army

The Salvation Army in the Black Country no doubt deserves a book all to itself. From the 1880s onwards, from the time of General Booth himself, it has had a presence in the Black Country, providing us with a legacy of memories, living traditions, and some splendid citadels.

Above: The Salvation Army Fort and Junior Soldier Barracks in Cradley Heath (1893 and 1900) are classics of Salvation Army architecture, but are now threatened with demolition to make way for the long-promised Cradley Heath bypass. The last services at this citadel were held on 1 August 2004. *(NW)*

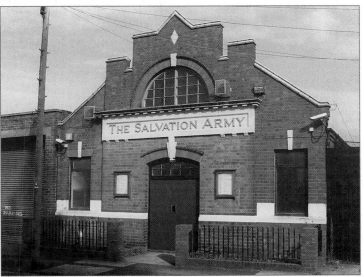

Right: The citadel in Blackheath. *(NW)*

Major and Mrs Snell, seated at the front of this picture, were leaving the Cradley Heath citadel on the night this photograph was taken – 23 May 2004 – and the band played for them before a presentation was made. *(NW)*

The Salvation Army band leads a Sunday School parade past Christ Church in the Lye, *c.* 1960. *(Bram Dunn collection)*

The Salvation Army Young People's Band outside their Church Street hall in the Lye, late 1920s. Bram Dunn is seated on the right. *(Bram Dunn collection)*

The Salvation Army Junior Songsters at Willenhall, 19 May 2002. *(NW)*

ACKNOWLEDGEMENTS

This book could not have been written without the considerable help of many individuals. I thank everybody who made me welcome in their chapel, or who was generous with their time and the resourses of their private archives and collections.

I particularly wish to thank the following, in alphabetical order:
Lloyd Abel, Sylvia Allcock, Ray Anstis, Ray Baggott, Peter Barnsley, John Barratt, Ron and Jean Beard, David Barker, Jill Berry, Albert Billingham, Peter and Frances Bloor, Barry Blunt, Margaret Bradley, Bob Broadfield, Beryl Cattell, Jerry Clarke, Madge and Ray Cole, Brian Conway, Bob Cooper, Roger Crombleholme, Harold and Iris Dale, Maureen Davis, Beryl and Cliff Davison, Marion and John Dunn, Edith Edgar, Helen Emery, Marlene Evans, Roy Evans, David Field, Colin Gardner, Kevin Gripton, Jill Guest, Alan Hallman, Thelma Hollinshead, Doug Hingley, Margaret Howells, John and Pam Hughes, John James, Maud and Easton Laird, John Lloyd, Desmond McDonald, Ron Moss, Raymond Oakley, David Oliver, Anthony Page, Joyce Parkes, Brian Payton, Anne Peters, G. B. Phillpott, Bill Poole, Jean Powell, Barbara Prettie, Alan Price, Evelyn Price, Ken Pritchard, Kathleen Rogers, Ted Smith, Wilf Smith, Ivy Timmington, Beryl Totney, Jasmine Vaughan, David Watts, Margaret Webb, Jean Weston, Albert Willetts, David Willetts, Graham Willets,Muriel Woodhouse, Ivan Williams, Cyril Wright, Norman Yardley. I have also received help from the *Express & Star*, and from the Local Archives and Local History Centres in Wolverhampton and Dudley.

Photographic credit is given in each caption. Where a picture is part of someone's collection all reasonable effort has been made to acknowledge the source of the photograph. The author is happy to make suitable redress in situations where someone is able to make a claim to ownership after publication. Photographs credited 'NW' are the work of the author.

I want to thank Terri Baker-Mills for accompanying me on visits to numerous chapels and for mopping my brow when the work intensified. This book was started without really stopping to think about just how many chapels once existed in the area! Whole areas of the Black Country were abandoned when it became clear that there was so much material in the districts covered in this volume. I hope, therefore, to produce a sequel to this book, and look forward to hearing from chapel enthusiasts in Wolverhampton, Walsall, Wednesbury, West Bromwich, Smethwick, Oldbury, Stourbridge and Dudley. I am sure there are also many gaps to fill in the districts covered in this volume.